W9-BKT-905

DATE DUE		
MAR 2 4 1998		
NOV 1 7 2000		
MAY 1 0 2010		

SHELTON STATE LIBRARY

DISCARDED

National Textbook Co
17.95

P.O. 62817

VGM Professional Careers Series

CAREERS
IN INTERNATIONAL
BUSINESS

EDWARD J. HALLORAN

DISCARDED

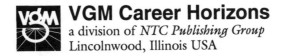

VGM Career Horizons
a division of *NTC Publishing Group*
Lincolnwood, Illinois USA

Cover photo courtesy of Thunderbird: The American Graduate School of International Management.

Library of Congress Cataloging-in-Publication Data

Halloran, Edward Joseph.
    Careers in international business/Ed Halloran.
        p. cm. — (VGM professional careers series)
    Includes bibliographical references.
    ISBN 0-8442-4492-9 (hard). — ISBN 0-8442-4493-7 (soft)
    1. International business enterprises—Vocational guidance.
I. Title. II. Series.
HD2755.5.H35   1995
331.7'02—dc20   95-565
                                     CIP

Published by VGM Career Horizons, a division of NTC Publishing Group
4255 West Touhy Avenue
Lincolnwood (Chicago), Illinois 60646-1975, U.S.A.
© 1996 by NTC Publishing Group. All rights reserved.
No part of this book may be reproduced, stored in a retrieval system,
or transmitted in any form or by any means,
electronic, mechanical, photocopying, recording or otherwise,
without the prior permission of NTC Publishing Group.
Manufactured in the United States of America.

5 6 7 8 9 0 VP 9 8 7 6 5 4 3 2 1

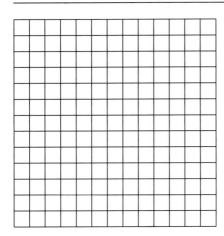

CONTENTS

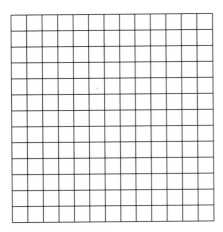

ABOUT THE AUTHOR

Edward J. Halloran holds degrees from Norwalk (CT) Community College, Columbia College, and Webster University. He is also a graduate of the American Academy of Dramatic Arts in New York City.

He has extensive corporate and consulting experience in the international sector and has lived and worked overseas.

Mr. Halloran has taught business, drama, and interpersonal relations courses at several institutions. For the past decade he has been on the faculty at Columbia College's Aurora, Colorado Extended Studies Center, where he teaches principles of management, principles of marketing, and global marketing.

His work with the Armed Forces Network during the 1960s while he was in the U.S. Air Force included action reporting from the Tonkin Gulf.

He also served for many years as a courtside announcer and off-court liaison at international team handball tournaments at the U.S. Olympic Training Center in Colorado Springs.

Mr. Halloran runs a multimedia production company in Denver, and, in 1993, he was awarded a bronze Cindy by the Association of Visual Communicators.

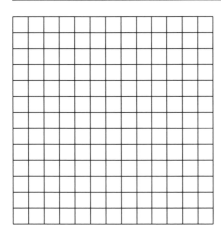

DEDICATION

In memory of Cathy and Jay Tarrant, and Dick Murdy.

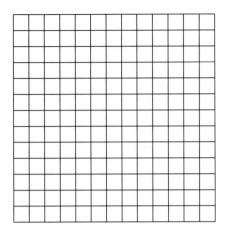

PREFACE

Simply put, trade between two nations is evaluated on the basis of per capita consumption of imports by the citizenry of each country. As a case in point, if the United States, with a population of roughly 250 million, consumes one hundred billion dollars worth of imports from a given country, while the second country, with a population of 125 million consumes fifty billion dollars worth of United States exports, trade is balanced.*

—Stephen B. Jamison

I selected the above quotation—from a keynote address on the common misconceptions that have served as barriers to truly free trade—because I believe that it makes an important point: It is unfair for the United States to expect smaller nations to match our expenditures, dollar for dollar. Unfortunately, too many people have taken the opposite tack, and that is that other nations owe us, and should at least spend as much on U.S. goods and services as we do on theirs, even if the countries are half our size, or even smaller.

Happily, we are learning, and NAFTA and GATT are positive steps toward more realistic trade policies.

Misconceptions will continue to exist for some time, however, and not only in the United States. For example, an American who wanted to go abroad and open an "American" restaurant might run into cultural biases, even in lands Americans have visited for many years.

I recently interviewed the owner of a Greek *taverna* located in Denver. He said that he was able to run an authentic Greek restaurant in the United States using virtually the same menu and music he would use if he were to operate a restaurant in Greece. However, he said that an "American" restaurant in Greece would most likely have to limit itself to fast food items because "That's what people think Americans eat all the time." Steaks, lobster, and Thanksgiving-style turkey dinners would not be considered "authentic" American fare.

---

* Stephen B. Jamison, "Leveling the Playing Field: Differing National Perspectives," presented to the Second International Conference on Global Business Environment and Strategy (1994), 4.

He also stated that anyone from the United States who wanted to do business in Greece would be well-advised to hire a consultant to help thread legal and bureaucratic mazes. It occurred to me that the average foreigner who came to the United States to start a business or sell a product would require similar assistance, particularly when it came to learning the ropes where local, state, and federal laws are concerned.

Again and again, as I conducted my research for this book, I heard the line, "If you want to do business overseas, get local help!" That works both ways: there are also opportunities for home-based "international" positions for U.S. citizens, particularly in a global economy that is looking to lower trade barriers and expand.

The positions will go to people who have prepared themselves properly, and that preparation is this book's primary concern.

P.S. I want to hear from you! Let me know how the principles discussed in this book have helped you to prepare for, enhance, or change your career. Your experiences and suggestions are vitally important to me as I update this book periodically in response to the ever-changing nature of international business.

Please write to:

Ed Halloran
Careers in International Business
c/o NTC Publishing Group
4255 West Touhy Avenue
Lincolnwood, IL 60646–1975

FOREWORD

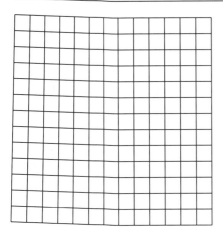

Throughout its history the United States has been able to dictate its desires, requiring others to change.

Our very continent was carved out of a rustic wilderness by our ability to think ahead and change our environment to what we wanted it to be. The native civilizations became a subculture as immigrants brought to the continent a new style of living, a different manner of dress, and a language that rapidly became the dominant tongue of the New World.

Following World Wars I and II U.S. influence reached into the farthest corners of the world. Products manufactured by the "Yankees," as we became known, were as familiar to the French as they were to the Chinese and as they were to the shoppers in Anytown, U.S.A.

Foreign markets opened rapidly as war-torn countries without the capability to produce turned to the cornucopia of American-made products to fill a void. Lucky Strike Cigarettes, Hershey Chocolates, Parker Writing Instruments, and Henry Ford's automobiles could now be purchased in London, Tokyo, and Berlin. American influence changed the world's way of living and ability to purchase. This happened so rapidly that the American marketing plan was merely to produce more and ship it overseas.

"Favored Nation Status" became a new slogan to help friendly nations sell some of their products in the United States. The after-war "Plans" proved to be successful and economies of nations in NATO (North Atlantic Treaty Organization) and SEATO (Southeast Asia Treaty Organization) became healthy. Demand for foreign-made products in this country exceeded all expectations, and the economic war for the Yankee dollar had begun.

As American factories were forced into financing social issues and increasing demands of labor, it became impractical to produce goods in this country, and our world dominance in manufacturing disappeared. Federal, state, and local government regulations imposed financial burdens that took many U.S. manufacturers out of a competitive posture with imported products. American production would never be the same—at least not in the American market.

Economic survival for the United States now means seeking new markets. We must sell what we do best—education, technology, and whatever manufacturing remains—to reach the purchasing power of the world. We can no longer "just produce more and ship it," we must market ourselves in competition with the world. We can no longer influence by demanding change. For the first time in our economic history, *we* must do the changing. We must learn the needs, wants, and desires of our global neighbors.

This global marketing requires international planning, culture and language education, and the access codes to these new markets. We can no longer just put Hershey candy bars on the shelf and know they will sell. We must be integrated into the social and economic structures of places such as Moscow, Bangkok, and Sidi Slimane. The demand for talent to serve these markets opens the greatest opportunity for this land since the days when our predecessors carved a nation out of the wilderness.

We are in a global economy, and we must prepare ourselves to serve it.

Raymond V. Morgan, M.A.S.
Vice President, Sales and Marketing
Barton Nelson, Inc.
Kansas City, Missouri

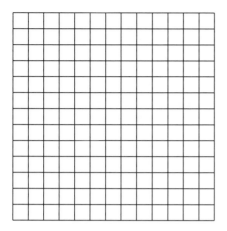

INTRODUCTION

There *are* jobs in the international sector for U.S. citizens, and all indications are that there will be many more as time goes by. However, most Americans* are ill-prepared to compete for these jobs.

The fact is, most foreigners are better educated (except, perhaps in the technical areas) than their American counterparts. First of all, foreigners tend to know their own language thoroughly, while functional illiteracy rates in the United States may run as high as 40 percent in some states. As a rule, Americans often do not write well, and this greatly reduces their employability in the international sector.

In addition to great facility in their own tongue, foreigners in the business world also speak one or more foreign languages fluently. Meanwhile, the average American who has "studied" another language is hard-pressed to get beyond observing, "My aunt's pen has fallen off the dresser."

English is the foreign language of choice for many people in the international business community, and they tend to speak it well. They are also fully conversant with geography and often know more about the world (including the United States) than do their American counterparts.

---

* For simplicity's sake, citizens of the United States are described throughout this book as "Americans." This is fine in a domestic setting, but keep in mind that people from Central and South America view themselves as Americans, too.

More accurately, we are "North Americans," and are referred to this way by our fellow Americans to the south. (In Spanish, the feminine term is *norteamericana*, and the masculine version is *norteamericano*.) A useful way to remind ourselves of this is to remember that the United States is a member of the Organization of *American* States.

While people from Europe, Asia, Africa, Australia, and even Canada are likely to refer to U.S. citizens as "Americans," people from other countries in our region may find us offensive if we arrogate this term for ourselves.

Americans can land international jobs, but to do so they are going to have to study harder on an ongoing basis. The world is in a constant state of political, economic, and social change, and people who want to succeed in what has become a global market for goods and services will need to keep abreast of these changes.

This book is designed to help Americans prepare to compete for international positions. Many, but not all of these jobs will be in sales and marketing. We will look at where the opportunities lie for a variety of positions, including traditional jobs, contract work, and increasingly, excellent opportunities for entrepreneurs.

Surprisingly, most of the opportunities for international work will be right here in the United States, and, in many cases, Americans will be working for foreign companies.

A well-prepared American has a great deal to offer a foreign firm, and challenging opportunities abound for people who are willing to continue to learn and grow. This book will provide a method for finding and keeping positions in the exciting world of international business.

HOW TO USE THIS BOOK

The mere fact that you are reading this book indicates that you have given at least a little thought to looking into career opportunities in the international sector. Although some chapters may be considered "stand-alones," I suggest reading them sequentially. This will help you determine if you are truly cut out for a career in international business, and, in the process, you will be exposed to other possibilities you may not have thought of.

Salary ranges have been left out on purpose, because if a given career does not appeal to you on its own merits, you are not going to be happy for very long, no matter how much money you are making.

When you are asked to answer questions, be honest with yourself. No one can help you unless *you* have determined what it is that you want to go after and what your strengths and shortcomings are.

Understand that you are reading a primer, and that you will need to do more research on your own. The sources that are mentioned throughout the book will provide you with a great deal of useful information.

Be open minded as you read the book and in your subsequent pursuit of knowledge. Too often in the past, Americans have tended to take a narrow look at the rest of the world. It was tasteless then, and it is economic suicide now, because we need other countries' business more than they need ours.

In short, it behooves us to become better citizens of the world and open ourselves to new possibilities. And why not? It is not only good business, it is enjoyable!

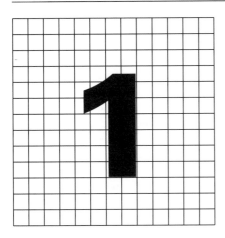

INTERNATIONAL BUSINESS: WHAT IS IN IT FOR YOU?

CHAPTER OBJECTIVES
Upon completion of this chapter, you should be able to:

1. Appreciate that we are dealing with a global economy
2. Understand the nature of your competition for international positions
3. Commit to a lifelong contract with yourself to continue to learn and grow

> As an international trading company, we remain firm proponents of world trade.... A world marketplace which fosters open competition, consumer choice and economic growth is important to the continued success of GrandMet.[1]
>
> —Sir Allen Sheppard, Chairman, GrandMet

In 1977, I attended a week-long management seminar. My company was a leader in the information industry and produced microfilm and microfiche using step and repeat planetary cameras. We were then on the cutting edge of technology, as we had already started preparing for our industry's next technological advance, computer-generated microfiche.

We were also the only firm represented that was engaged in any significant amount of international trade. The other companies who were represented at the seminar were quite content with their domestic business, and their managers were almost patronizing when they called our efforts "interesting." Two of these companies were enormously successful, and were the stars of the seminar.

Now, nearly two decades later, my old company is firmly established in the international marketplace and is already working with optical discs and CD-ROM. Meanwhile, one of the two star companies from that not-so-long-ago gathering is barely surviving, and the other, after nearly going under, is looking to international business to save it.

THE GLOBAL VILLAGE

The term *global village* has been with us for some time now. The world's governments have begun to acknowledge that we are in a single, global economy, which is *market driven*. NAFTA and GATT are two recent admissions that we are all inextricably intertwined with one another in a single

---

[1] GrandMet, *1993 Annual Report*, 6.

marketplace, and that trade restrictions are, ultimately, self-defeating. So, ever so slowly, we are moving in the direction of truly free trade.

Protectionism withers in the face of economic reality. If what a company is doing is not cost-effective, ultimately, even its domestic market will shop elsewhere. The proliferation of Japanese cars in the U.S. market is a good case in point. For many years, the Japanese made cars for less money than their American counterparts—even during periods when Japanese autoworkers were being paid more than were U.S. autoworkers—because Japanese factories were, to the greatest extent possible, using industrial robots.

In addition to effecting economies in the workplace, the Japanese were more responsive to the needs of the American market, making changes in vehicle size and style as the market dictated. Meanwhile, American automakers criticized the Japanese and asked, "Why don't *they* buy *our* cars?" The "they" actually included not only the Japanese, but also people in the United States.

On the domestic front, people were buying foreign cars because they were sick of Detroit's gas guzzlers. Meanwhile, people in Japan were not buying even the most prestigious U.S. cars because in Japan, as in England, the steering wheel is on the right side of the car, and U.S. automakers were attempting to sell them typical American cars with the steering wheels on the left! We as a nation paid for this error with an unfavorable balance of trade.

Although the automotive industry's criticism of Japan was largely irrational, the Japanese have maintained restrictive barriers against foreign— chiefly U.S.—goods (including agricultural products) that are less expensive and better than their Japanese rivals' offerings. This protectionism has hurt Japan, and slowly, accommodations are being made. But the process is painful because in Japan, as in other countries, powerful domestic groups such as unions and industry associations aggressively attempt to maintain trade barriers.

The trade barriers are, however, gradually disappearing, and major concessions have been made in recent years. You have only to look at the Japanese-owned factories in the United States to understand that we are in a time of significant change, and that we need to prepare ourselves to deal with this change.

Ray Morgan, the international marketer who wrote the introduction to this book, made the following comments about protectionism in a recent letter to me:

> Protecting the American automobile industry by permitting the engines to be made in the Orient, the bodywork in Mexico and then installing Canadian-made seats in Detroit to qualify as an "American Made Product" puts the cause of international marketing and "Free Trade" back into the 17th century. … Manufacturers must produce a superior product with quality that will withstand competition from around the world....We must think global markets, but first remove the invisible barriers.

Just as American Express was pulled into the world of international banking when immigrants sent money orders that were meant to be used in the United States back to their families in Europe, more and more American firms have discovered that new markets are opening up to them overseas, which leads to more and more opportunities for Americans to work in the international sector.

The growth in international marketing due to changes abroad will create more positions based in the United States for individuals interested in international marketing. However, entry-level positions abroad are few.... Usually, companies hire foreign nationals for most positions in foreign branches.[2]

In addition to adhering, in some cases, to foreign governments' dictates that the bulk of the employees of U.S. firms doing business there be locals, there are other valid reasons for not sending inexperienced Americans abroad. As a senior executive in a large firm's international department told me, "By letting local nationals serve as our primary contacts abroad, I eliminate the risk of having an American approach a prospective client in the wrong way. I let the locals set things up, and I don't have to worry about their telling the wrong kind of joke, or being too pushy. Overseas, as a general rule, people want to get to know representatives of commercial firms as people first, before business is ever discussed. Most Americans have a difficult time dealing with this and, in many cases, the cultural and linguistic knowledge required to open doors abroad requires many years of study, indeed, you might even say a lifetime."

I asked him, "Once opened, is there a place inside the door for an American?" He replied, "Yes, if he or she is an expert at something such as technical knowledge or finance. Using the local nationals on an ongoing basis to smooth the way for them, Americans can make significant contributions."

Reasonable fluency and continued study of the host country's language or languages is virtually mandatory. This does not mean that fluent Americans will ultimately reach a point at which they can negotiate deals unaided—the individuals who can do this are rare because of legal, linguistic, and cultural complexities—but continued improvement in the host country's tongue shows an appreciation for the country's culture and is greatly appreciated.

A woman who brokers deals in Eastern Europe told me, "Down through the years, through frequent travel and formal study, I've turned my high school German and a smattering of Polish into a fair degree of fluency. I still make laughable grammatical errors, but the people I'm transacting with are trying out their English on me, and sometimes it's pretty funny, so we laugh together, and keep on trying.... I'll always need interpreters for hammering out the details of contracts, but my continued improvement in spoken languages has solidified my business relationships."

---

[2] Stair, Lila B. and Dorothy Dombkowski, *Careers in Business*. Lincolnwood, IL: VGM Career Horizons, 1992, 108.

The people who succeed in the international sector "know what they *don't* know," and do something about it. Opportunities abound for Americans who are flexible enough to work in the international sector. If you are interested, your expertise in a given area may well be in demand.

Speaking of expertise, how well do you know your *own* country? In a recent Gallup Poll, 50 percent of the respondents could not find New York State on a map.[3]

Which 50 percent are *you* in? In the following section you will meet a young woman from Europe whose knowledge of the United States, its geography, language, and history would put many Americans to shame. And, most important of all, she "knows what she doesn't know" and continues to pursue knowledge.

AN EXAMPLE OF A FOREIGN "COMPETITOR"

Juncal Pereda (Guijarro) is a young university student in Spain. She is an exceptional yet not atypical example of a foreign "competitor." Juncal has twice delayed her own in-country education to study in the United States. She lived with the author's family on the first occasion, when she went through the 12th grade at a local high school as an exchange student. She had belonged to the English Club at her school in Spain, and was already quite fluent when she arrived in the United States. She finished fourth in her graduating class and was accepted into the National Honor Society.

Along the way, she played varsity soccer, skied regularly with the school's club, served as a manager and scorekeeper for the basketball team, and was an active member of the physics club.

Juncal would be an exceptional person anywhere, but there are a great many foreign nationals just like her, and many of them are anxious to work in the international sector.

While she lived with us, Juncal read avidly, and was able to comprehend and discuss detailed novels from the United States and England. Nevertheless, she was back in the United States two years later to attend business classes at a university in California. She said, "I'm majoring in business administration, and eventually, I want to work for a U.S. company in Europe. So, this year, I'm working on my business English and learning American marketing concepts. Next year, when I return home, I really need to work on my French so I'll be a more valuable asset to a prospective employer." This additional training in the United States will delay her completing the requirements for her degree for a year, just as her high school experience delayed her entry into the university, but she feels that the trade of time for knowledge is well worth while.

---

[3] Photo caption, *Rocky Mountain News*, May 17, 1994, 5A.

ASSESSING YOUR KNOWLEDGE

The following questions will help you assess your knowledge in areas important to a career in international business:

1. What foreign country or countries would you like to work in?
2. How well do you speak the language?
3. How sound is your knowledge of the country's physical, human, and economic geography?
4. How extensive is your knowledge of the country's customs, traditions, and history?
5. How does conducting business there differ from the way it is done in the United States?
6. Make an honest assessment of your answers to the previous questions. At this point, how desirable are you as a potential representative of a U.S. firm in the country or countries you have mentioned?
7. Go back and answer questions 2 through 6, assessing your knowledge of the United States.

ACTION PLAN

Not everyone has the time and the means to follow Juncal's example to the letter. However, there are things you can do right where you are now.

1. List the places where you can study the language or languages you need. Note time commitments and costs.
2. Write a two- or three-page report on how business is transacted in a country that appeals to you. Compare and contrast the country's customs with those of the United States.
3. Write another two- or three-page report outlining the economic future of the country you wrote about in the previous report. What is the country's economic outlook? Who is likely to do well there?
4. Make a list of at least five U.S. firms that are doing business in the country you have been writing about. If these firms are publicly held corporations, contact them and request their annual reports and 10K forms.
5. Having read the reports you obtain, pick the most desirable company and draft a letter to the head of its international sector. In it, tell the head why you feel that the company is a good place for you to work. Indicate what you have studied, both formally and informally, and outline your plans for future studies. Lay the draft of the letter aside for a few days. Then, read it and ask yourself if *you* would give the writer of that letter a follow-up call had such a letter arrived at your office. If the answer is yes, proof the letter carefully and send it to the

company with your resume. If your answer is no, ask yourself *why* you are not a person they would like to talk to at this point, and how you can become such a person.

A COMMITMENT TO LEARNING

There is a growing demand for Americans to work in the international sector as entrepreneurs, contract workers, representatives, consultants, or that rapidly vanishing breed, the "regular" employees. Success goes to people who are willing to make a lifelong commitment to the pursuit of knowledge. This pursuit begins by deciding to expand your horizons starting now.

A good place to begin is with looking at major differences between the United States and other countries. Peggy Kenna and Sondra Lacy have written a delightful series of business overviews for Passport Books. Their fast-moving paperbacks, *Business France, Business China, Business Germany, Business Japan, Business Mexico,* and *Business Taiwan* provide a good look at how things are done in the host country and include excellent issue-by-issue comparisons with the American approach. Their presentations afford us a highly instructive opportunity to see ourselves through the eyes of others. Their discussion of China serves as a particularly good example:

> The Chinese view time in very long terms; their civilization and their country is over 2,000 years old.... they look at the long (i.e., 500 years) view. They don't understand the concept of doing things promptly and feel Americans are much too impatient. The Chinese will often use this impatience against Americans in negotiating with them.[4]

Our impatience hurts us again and again because, no matter where we do business around the world, the people with whom we come in contact have a different concept of time. They often value periods of silent reflection, while we are in a hurry to get on with things and, instead of considering silence to be productive, we assume that the other party's response to us is negative. To break the perceived logjam, we offer a concession. That is the disadvantage Kenna and Lacy are talking about in the above quote.

The late W. Edwards Deming, the Total Quality guru, found a receptive audience for his message in Japan. He was committed to pursuing perfection on a lifelong basis. This sat very well with people in every area of endeavor in Japan, but in America, Deming's homeland, the idealization of "quick fixes" held sway for many years. Meanwhile, in achieving quality, Japanese manufacturers were far surpassing their American counterparts.

After several decades, it finally occurred to U.S. firms that maybe there *was* something to total quality management after all.

Many firms imitated Deming, while others sought his counsel. Successful companies who committed themselves to the bulk of his principles and kept

---

[4] Peggy Kenna and Sondra Lacy, *Business China* (Lincolnwood, IL: Passport Books, 1994), 30.

working on improving the quality of their goods and services benefited from the Deming method. Others, in the words of a manager who was interviewed by one of my students, "Tried that total quality stuff for a while, but it just didn't work!"

If you are interested in a career in the international sector, be prepared to commit yourself wholeheartedly for the long term. This book does not offer any quick fixes because in order to work effectively in international settings, you have to be a perpetual student—not only of other cultures, but of your own as well.

This lifelong pursuit of knowledge is frequently fascinating and, on occasions, frustrating. There will be many challenging moments throughout your working life, but each one will present you with an opportunity to learn and grow. The knowledge that you are still evolving should encourage you greatly because it means that, while others have dropped out, you are still open to exciting new possibilities.

Your competitors will be found both here at home and abroad. In either case, they are individuals who have committed themselves to preparing for *careers,* which means that they are looking at things from a long-term perspective. In order to compete with them, you will need to make a similar commitment, as expressed in the following "contract."

YOUR FIRST "CONTRACT"

Please read the following contract. It is the starting point for your quest for a true career in the international sector. Like any other first step, many surprises will follow. If you are serious about a career in international business, you will greet the surprises as exciting challenges and do your best to meet them. If you can commit to this learning process, it is likely that you will succeed in international business.

I promise myself that I will keep an open mind as I survey the international sector for career possibilities. This will include acknowledging the fact that I may be deficient in one or more aspects and then doing something positive to bring myself up to an acceptable level. I realize that I will be dealing with different customs, traditions, and languages, and I promise that I will learn to appreciate these differences as valid alternatives to my own culture. Finally, I pledge that I will continue to strive to learn more about my own culture as well as the ones I will be dealing with throughout the course of my career.

_____

Signature and Date

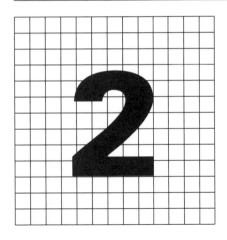

EXPANDING YOUR HORIZONS

CHAPTER OBJECTIVES

After reading this chapter, you should:

1. Have a better appreciation of the need to learn more about other cultures
2. Have the opportunity to implement a plan of action to start your learning process

International marketers need to be aware of each foreign market's cultural environment. A *culture* consists of a group of people sharing a distinctive heritage. This heritage teaches behavior standards, language, life-styles and goals.... A firm unfamiliar with or insensitive to a foreign culture may try to market goods or services that are unacceptable to or misunderstood by that culture.

—Joel R. Evans and Barry Berman[1]

We can extrapolate from the advice given to corporations in the preceding quote and apply it to the individual. Whether we are talking about a consulting agreement, an entrepreneurial venture, or seeking a position with a company that does business internationally, to what extent do we as individuals appreciate the nuances of other cultures?

In this chapter, we will explore avenues to learning more about other people and their values. We will also look at career areas that are opening up for Americans who are properly prepared.

THE IMPORTANCE OF STUDYING LANGUAGE AND CULTURE

Although some foreign languages are currently "hotter" than others in the international marketplace, a working knowledge of *any* additional language is very helpful. What is critical is that we be flexible and realize that we should not limit ourselves solely to that language and the country or countries where it is spoken.

An international marketing executive told me that a lot of Americans tend to sell themselves short in this regard. He cited a recent resume and cover letter he had received: "The writer had two years of German in high school and two more in college. The cover letter went on and on about the writer's appreciation for Germany and its heritage, although nowhere in the letter or resume was any indication that he had ever even visited the country!" The

[1] Joel R. Evans and Barry Berman, *Marketing*, 6th ed. (New York: Macmillan, 1992), 179.

executive added, "The letter talked about how he'd like to 'represent' us in Germany, and left the door closed to any other possibilities. I tossed it."

And why not? Let's look at where the writer went wrong:

1. Focusing on Germany *only*. As the executive said, "What if we're not hiring anyone to work in Germany?"
2. Claiming expertise concerning a given country, without having actually been there! (Even if the writer had only been to Germany once, as part of a tour group, the trip could have been referred to something like this: "In addition to studying the language, I have traveled extensively throughout the country.")
3. Failing to see that having mastered the rudiments of one foreign language would make the study of other languages somewhat easier.

A better approach would have included researching the company more thoroughly before contacting the executive. If the writer had done his homework, he would have learned that the firm's management hired local nationals to represent them overseas, but that they were looking for entry-level people in their international department—people who had studied a foreign language and who were willing to learn one or more other languages at the company's expense. International travel would have eventually ensued, but not until the company felt that the individual had been properly trained.

Self-help books, tapes, and seminars urge us to make the most out of what we know. The person whom we have been talking about would have been well advised, after conducting his research, to write something along these lines:

> I have completed four years of German, two at the college level. I am fluent, and constantly working for improvement. While I would prefer working with this language, studying it has proven to me that I have a facility for languages and that I enjoy learning about other cultures. So, I am open to other possibilities if there is no vacancy in your German operation.

That kind of approach would have earned the writer an interview, which is the purpose of sending a cover letter and resume, and he would have been in the running for a position. Instead, he didn't make it past the initial screening.

Learning about another culture before you attempt to do business in that country is vital:

> The most important rule in living and working internationally is: *Know before you go!* It is your responsibility to know and understand the principal rules and institutions of your chosen country. These countries don't expect you to know or understand all of their cultural nuances. They do expect that you make *an effort* to know and respect their laws and culture. The trick in international business is to get off an airplane, find your way to your hotel, client's office and the bathroom. Complete your business and leave without creating an international incident.[2]

---

[2] Craig W. Christianson, *New ReView,* June 1994, 6.

Studying the language is a good place to begin, as it shows the people with whom you come in contact that you are willing to make the effort to learn the most basic part of their culture.

Greeting people in their own language opens the door to meaningful communication. By taking the time and making the effort to study a language, you have expanded your horizons. After all, if there is more than one way of saying something, then there is also more than one way of looking at things. I remember when I was stationed in the Orient during my time in the U.S. Air Force. An officer who conducted our introductory briefing said, "You will doubtless find our hosts' way of doing things somewhat 'strange' compared to the way you were raised. Keep in mind that this culture has evolved over thousands of years to meet the needs of its people, and that it is as valid to them as our own system is to us." During the years that I spent living overseas, I never forgot that briefing, and I devoted myself to learning everything I could about the region and its people.

My efforts did not go unnoticed, and people approached me and provided me with books and insights that further enhanced my appreciation for their culture and made me enjoy the privileged opportunity I had to live and work in another country. This, in turn, opened my mind to other possibilities around the world, and I embarked on what has turned out to be a lifelong study of how various cultures cope with life on this planet.

HOW TO LEARN A LANGUAGE

The thought of studying another language is somewhat daunting to many, if not most people. The idea of learning grammar is absolutely frightening!

Happily, today's emphasis is on learning to speak first, and then gradually learning the relevant structures, which will enable you to build on your existing knowledge and begin to express your thoughts.

The best way to learn a language is to study it with other people, under the guidance of a skilled instructor. Schools, colleges, and adult education courses abound in our society, and courses tend to be scheduled so that virtually anyone who wants to learn can find a convenient course.

The next best thing is to use audio- and/or videotapes, preferably those that provide more than one voice and use real-life situations. Passport Books' "Just Listen 'n Learn" business language series is excellent. Their audiotapes use a variety of voices (which gets you used to "living" the language, rather than simply parroting the words of a single "master") and deal with day-to-day activities.

Another advantage to using this series is that the tapes were recorded by people from the United Kingdom. In the English sections, you will hear expressions that may be unfamiliar to you, even though you speak the "same" language. This is a useful reminder that, even in English-speaking countries, linguistic and cultural differences exist.

Whether you are using these tapes or others, (and there are many good ones on the market), you have to realize that you only will begin to master a language when you have committed yourself to work with it on a regular, preferably daily, basis. This requires discipline, and acknowledging that every now and again you will hit a plateau and not seem to be making progress at the rate you were at first. Don't get discouraged. There will be peaks and valleys in language study, particularly after you have gotten beyond the present tense and begin to express abstract thoughts. At that point, you will be a little frustrated because you realize how much you *don't* know. Don't sell yourself short, however, because you have actually gained the ability to think in and use the language to express yourself, not merely to order a room or a meal. With continued practice and study, greater fluency will inevitably ensue.

WHY LANGUAGE STUDY IS NECESSARY

One language instructor claims that only 5 percent of the general population is truly bilingual. His definition of the term is that the speaker has equal fluency, topic for topic, in two languages. When I look at it that way, I recognize that, although I can read a newspaper, order a meal, and rent a hotel room in French, I am far from being truly bilingual.

Too often, Americans tend to feel that a smattering of a foreign language qualifies them to represent a firm in a country where that language is spoken. Nothing could be further from the truth.

Let's go back to the letter from the young man who had studied German in high school and college. It is likely that the four years of study enabled him to handle day-to-day basics, largely in the present tense. He would probably be able to fight his way through a newspaper article and understand the bulk of it. All of this is quite admirable, but it is a far cry from conducting business, which, after all, frequently includes highly technical discussions in the past and future tenses. This young man is in no way equipped to deal in German with someone who, in addition to being a native speaker, may hold one or more degrees.

So, why even study a language at all? The odds are, you will never be truly bilingual, and fluency will take years. As a matter of fact, I once mentioned to a professor at a world-renowned school that I had been shocked to learn that only about 50 percent of the schools that offer a major or a concentration in international business require students to take a foreign language. He replied, "Well, why should they?... [If] someone studies French, and then they don't go to a French-speaking country, they've wasted their time! Besides, English is the official language of international business, and anyone who wants to do business with us already speaks it!"

It is difficult to decide where to begin evaluating the professor's words and their underlying assumptions. Let's start with the phrase, "they've wasted their time."

Studying another language, *any* language, causes us to grow intellectually. In the process, we learn about another people and their approach to life. It is important to know where those with whom we hope to do business are "coming from," and learning about their language and culture can teach us a great deal.

Even if we have to learn another language (at our employer's expense), having already learned one new language, we are most likely going to be better students the second time around.

The professor also stated, "English is the official language of business." Yes, and as the professor pointed out, people who want to do business with us do tend to speak it, and they generally speak it well. If it is expected that they will learn our language, why should we not be expected to learn theirs?

Well, as our trade deficits clearly indicate, international markets seem to be finding other suppliers—suppliers represented by people who appreciate their customers' cultures and who have learned at least the basics of the relevant language(s). Jingoism should have died a long time ago. People who carry over the superior attitude displayed by "ugly Americans," who held sway when we were the only alternative in the marketplace, will find themselves addressed in English by potential customers and, more often than not, what will be said is a very polite "No, thank you."

Practice what you have learned. Find a language circle (ask your teacher, check the classifieds or, if need be, start one yourself). Read books, newspapers, and periodicals in your foreign language and, whenever possible, eat in restaurants where that language is used on the menu and spoken by the staff.

MORE WAYS TO EXPAND YOUR CULTURAL HORIZONS

While we are on the subject of food, a simple way to expand your horizons is to try new things on a regular basis. Americans who are nonjudgmental when it comes to eating ethnic foods rapidly become popular when they are in a foreign land. People will open up new avenues for learning when they feel at ease with you. This not only heightens your enjoyment of being in a foreign country (or with a subculture in the United States, for that matter), but it also tends to strengthen personal ties, which can carry the day when it comes to landing jobs and/or contracts.

Music is another important element of any culture, and virtually every country has its own dances. Folk dancing groups abound, even in rural areas in the United States, and they are a great way to meet people and learn more about a country. In addition to the music and dancing, group members may discuss the cultures whose dances they are learning and sample ethnic foods and beverages.

Albums and videotapes will also help you to gain a greater appreciation for a country, and they will expand your vocabulary as well. So will films. Major cities tend to have theaters where foreign films are shown, and, very often, colleges and universities show foreign films, and the viewings are open to the public.

Language and cultural training do not have to cost a fortune. They also do not need to be taken for credit. Community schools, "free" universities, adult education programs, and organizations such as the Alliance Française offer low-cost classes as well as films, books, magazines, and newspapers. These organizations also sponsor events to celebrate major holidays in other countries, which are enjoyable learning experiences.

In short, there are plenty of low-cost or no-cost opportunities for you to learn and grow and have fun in the process.

CONDUCTING BUSINESS IN DIFFERENT CULTURES

Each nation presents a different selling proposition. In order to sell yourself first, and eventually your company's products, you need to know how business is conducted in that country.

Our way of doing business in the United States works very well for us. We tend to get on a first-name basis very quickly, and then we immediately begin the business negotiation. We are bottom-line oriented and, because "time is money," we do not "waste" time with a lot of "meaningless chatter."

We also do not feel comfortable with long periods of silence. That is not a problem in the United States, because the person across the desk from us does not like silence either, and is ready to begin talking the moment we stop.

We think at several times the rate of speech, so we are always busy, deciding what we will say next, just as soon as the other person stops talking. Instead of listening to what a person is saying, we concentrate on our next snappy line and listen for the silence that will provide us with the opportunity to say it.

People in other countries feel uncomfortable with our haste to transact. They also tend to be considerably more formal than we are and to value their privacy.

Silence, to a foreigner, is not an embarrassing bit of what radio people call "dead air." Rather, it is a time for reflecting upon what has already been said and formulating a thoughtful reply before speaking again.

LANGUAGE IS THE KEY TO A CULTURE

Again, language is the key to a culture. The more time we devote to learning a language, the more we will appreciate the heritage, customs, and traditions of the country we wish to do business with.

Remember, our own language is constantly evolving, and our growth as English speakers should be lifelong. That being the case, we need to be patient with ourselves when it comes to studying another language.

Take the example of a person who, although fluent in French, would not attempt to negotiate a contract in that language. Even so, the ability to discuss current events, art, and philosophy in French would give a distinct advantage over someone who barely speaks the language or does not speak it at all. At contract time, an attorney and an interpreter would be called in, but the point is, without the earlier conversations on other matters—although seemingly unrelated—it is unlikely that business would have resulted.

The mark of truly educated persons is not how much they know, but their awareness of how much they have yet to learn. A good education cannot teach you everything. What it can do is provide you with the tools to pursue knowledge on a lifelong basis. Interesting people are those who continue to learn and grow and, in the international sector, the more vigorously you are pursuing knowledge, the more intriguing people will find you, and the more respect they will have for you. Once that happens, meaningful business relationships inevitably ensue.

ACTION PLAN

What follows is a series of steps designed to help you learn about another culture. This example uses France, although you can easily apply this action plan to any other culture.

Week One: Check out a series of language tapes from your local library. Memorize basic greetings and the names for your favorite foods and beverages. Also, while you are at the library, secure a copy of Theodore Zeldin's *The French,* (which is in English) and read any two chapters that interest you.

Week Two: Continue to work with the language tapes, concentrating on the sections dealing with ordering food and drink. Revisit the library and/or bookseller and leaf through a periodical. *Paris Match* is a good choice. Make a list of the words that have the same spelling in English as they do in French. Try to get the gist of the articles and advertisements.

Week Three: Return the tapes to the library. Visit a French restaurant, and try out your vocabulary as you order.

Week Four and Beyond: Arrange to enroll in a basic French course. If there is a waiting period, fill in the time by listing French words that have made their way intact into our language (this will keep you from experiencing *ennui*), including the names of cities, rivers, lakes, and so on. Revisit the French restaurant, and try preparing various French dishes at home. Check out recordings in French (Edith Piaf, Charles Aznavour, "Tales of Hoffman" in the original language, and so on), and videotapes of films and travelogues. Whenever a French film is being shown locally, go. And, if there is a branch of the Alliance Française nearby, join.

What you have done is to put yourself in motion, to begin to learn about the French language and culture. Music, literature, film, food: these are all critical elements of a culture, and they are fun to experiment with.

By taking this course of action, you are opening yourself to new experiences and possibilities, and you are making yourself more employable in the international sector.

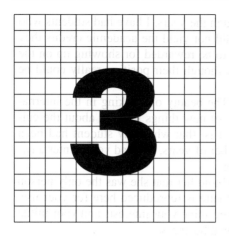

TRAINING FOR A CAREER IN INTERNATIONAL BUSINESS

CHAPTER OBJECTIVES

Upon completion of this chapter, you should be able to:

1. Identify the educational and experiential requirements you will need for positions in the international sector
2. Determine which type of training is likely to be most productive for you
3. Map out a plan for acquiring the credentials you will need
4. Take the first steps toward reaching your goal

WHAT DO YOU WANT TO DO?

A student said to me recently, "I've been reading the classifieds in the papers, and I can't find any jobs that appeal to me. Is there a better place to look?" I told her that there are lots of places to look, but it helped to know first what she was looking for. She replied, "A better job."

I asked what she meant by "better." It turned out that she really had not thought things through. In fact, that had been a pattern throughout her working life. She had drifted from job to job, leaving each to take a "better" position that turned out to be either the same as the one she had left, or even a little worse.

Personnel pro Gwen Lawton says that is common. "When I look at many applications under the heading, 'Reason for Leaving,' it will say, 'To take a better job.' When I assess what they left, and what they went to, it quickly becomes apparent that they were making a lateral move at best and, often taking a half step or so down."

People frequently become restless on the job. For any number of reasons, the job is no longer satisfying, and we want to do something else, sometimes almost anything else. This is not surprising, because many jobs, even glamorous ones, are quite repetitive.

Years ago, I attended a briefing on awarding college academic credit for working experience. The gentleman conducting the session said, "Someone tells us they have 17 years of experience in the electronics industry, and they want credit for it. Our question to them is, is it 17 years of different experiences, or 17 times one?"

The point is well taken. Down through the years, I have had students who fumed that their years of experience did not yield the academic credits they had expected. They seemed to expect to be rewarded for showing up on the job each day for all those years, even though their position really could be described as "times one."

Many positions truly are routine. (The beauty of working in the international sector is that you never run out of new things to learn about the culture(s) you are dealing with.) The fact is, that while my student had been working at a variety of jobs for a number of years, she had yet to enter a *career* field, and had simply been drifting.

I drafted a questionnaire for her and told her that she was the only person who knew the answers. That questionnaire is reproduced here for your use. You will find it a convenient way to determine your interests and your initial qualifications for a career in international business.

1. Where do you want to be ten years from now?
   - Position
   - Geographic location
   - Salary range
2. Where are you now in relation to those long-term goals?
   - Position (factor in education and experience)
   - Geographic location
   - Salary range
3. Can you attain the aforementioned goals by remaining with your present employer?
4. Can you attain some of those goals if you stay with your employer for a while longer?
   - If yes, which goals?
   - How long will you have to remain with your employer in order to reach these preliminary goals?
5. If there is no chance for reaching any of the goals by staying where you are, should you remain while you gather educational credits?
   - If the answer is yes, what do you need to do next in order to get started on bolstering your educational credentials?
   - If the answer is no, what is your plan for getting into a position that is more conducive to attaining your goals?

The following detailed questions will help you to further explore your career options.

Position: When you project yourself forward ten years and visualize your ideal career, do you honestly know:

1. What do people in that field *do* all day long?
2. What education and experience do they need to qualify?
3. What are the future projections for that field?

Geographic Location: Precisely where do you want to be living ten years from now? Answer these questions:

1. What firms that are likely employers are located there?
2. How likely are the above firms to remain (and expand)?
3. Who will you be competing with for employment?
4. How comfortable would your significant other(s) be living there?

Salary Range:

1. What does your dream position pay?
2. What do you have to do in return?
   - Relocation: How many moves, and how frequently do you have to move?
   - Travel: Where, how often, and for how long?
3. Is it worth it to you? To your significant others?

You also need to consider how many hours you will be putting in even while you are at home. Do these hours allow you sufficient time for your personal life? If not, you may want to rethink your goals.

My student found the questions on significant others particularly relevant. She said, "A few years ago when I was single, I would have been willing to relocate just about anywhere. But now I'm married with two kids. My husband likes his job, and we like our house. While I really want to work in international business, I don't want to move!" Happily, her state, Colorado, has many opportunities for her to work with an international firm or to serve as a contract rep for a foreign firm, so she can be based in her own home city. However, travel is a must. That did not pose a problem for my student—provided, she said, "that I'm not away *all* the time."

Travel requirements vary from one position and organization to another. I once had a corporate marketing job that had me flying all over the United States and Canada. I was on the road three weeks out of every four. It was a tremendous experience, but I gave up a great deal in return for it. Putting it mildly, I didn't have a life outside of the corporate world. For a time, that did not matter, but it does matter to me now, and I have no interest in doing such extensive traveling again for any amount of money.

EDUCATION

What are the educational requirements for the career you have chosen? Education options include junior and technical colleges, four-year undergraduate programs, and graduate programs. In each case, it is important to choose your school carefully.

Choosing a School

As a prospective student, you are valuable to schools, so be certain that you shop around before enrolling in a program. School guidance counselors and reference librarians can help to steer you in the right direction in choosing a school, and the schools you are thinking of applying to should be able to give you information concerning financial aid. The list of reference books in the "Action Plan" at the end of this chapter will also prove helpful.

In addition to your library research, check out the school through its graduates and their employers. Schools should not have anything to hide when it comes to this, so feel free to ask them for a list of graduates, including recent ones, and contacts in the personnel departments of prospective employers who have hired graduates of the school.

Don't be shy about this! Your career is at stake, after all, and you are also about to commit to a year or more of training at the school.

Ask the school's graduates the following questions:

1. How important was your training at your school in terms of landing you a job?
2. How relevant is that training in terms of what you are actually doing now?
3. How well prepared are you for the future as a result of your training?
4. If you had it to do over again, would you go to the same school or another one? Why?

Ask personnel representatives of firms employing the school's graduates these questions:

1. How have graduates from this school performed on the job?
2. How relevant was the training they brought to their first jobs with you?
3. Are there other schools of the same type that you respect more? Which one(s)?
4. Do you foresee an ongoing need for more graduates for positions with your company?

Be aware that many schools will pressure you to enroll, and that they make all sorts of promises. *Take your time in making your choice!* The choice of a school is an important career decision.

The following "horror story" illustrates the need to take care in choosing a school: A few years ago, I was offered a job as a part-time marketing instructor. I was all set to accept, but then I was told, "And you'll also be teaching accounting." When I pointed out that, while I had some training in the area, I did not consider myself to be qualified to teach accounting, I was told that the position required teaching both subjects and, after all, "The answers to all the problems are in the instructor's manual, so you'll be all set." I responded, "That's all well and good, but I'm not certain that the answers to students' questions are in my head!"

I refused the job. I did ask, though, what they planned to do. The director said, "We have resumes on file from several accounting teachers and I'm sure that one of them will be willing to teach marketing, too, so there's no problem." I pointed out that marketing and accounting are frequently in strong opposition to each other in the corporate world, and that two teachers were really necessary in order to present both perspectives. The director replied, "Oh, that doesn't really matter all that much!" That is precisely the type of school you need to avoid. Taking the time to check references thoroughly can help you to steer clear of unethical institutions.

The best universities and colleges constantly assess their programs and strive to be more responsive to the needs of the business world. Be leery of schools that are not evolving, because the dynamics in the global marketplace are constantly changing as technology advances and trade barriers fall.[1]

Junior Colleges and Technical Schools

Do you need additional technical knowledge? If so, a junior college or technical school may be right for you. Both degree and certificate programs are available.

A word about two-year degrees for undergraduates: Generally speaking, people from other countries value education a great deal. Frequently, I am asked by undergraduate students if they should complete the requirements for an associate's degree, or just concentrate on the four-year degree. My advice is, if you can get a two year degree on your way to a B.A. or B.S., do it. In many cases, our students' tuition is being paid by their employers. When times get tough, education budgets are frequently slashed, so it pays to get a degree after your name as quickly as possible.

Although the completed credit hours may be exactly the same, there is a considerable perceptual difference between having "two years of college" and holding a two-year degree. The former description sounds like the person has not made up his or her mind yet about a career, while the latter indicates that the person finishes what he or she starts and has successfully completed the requirements for an accredited degree.

Four-Year Undergraduate Programs

A bachelor's degree is frequently a minimum requirement for people who are seeking to enter career fields. This is particularly true in the international sector. Earning a degree indicates serious commitment, and the ability to complete a rigorous program. Obeying the dictum "Be an expert," your undergraduate pursuits may be devoted to something quite specific, such as accounting or computer information systems. If that is the case, please be sure to include at least one foreign language among your electives.

---

[1] This issue is addressed effectively by Suzanne L. MacLachlan in her article "Business Schools Scrambling to Stay Current" (*Christian Science Monitor,* April 4, 1994, 7). The article is well worth reading, as it makes a convincing case for the need for change.

A representative undergraduate program is Columbia College's International Business Emphasis for students who are going to earn a B.A. or a B.S. in Business Administration. The program requires a minimum of 18 hours from the following courses, at least 12 of which must be upper-level courses (numbered 300 to 400):

Two 400-level courses are required: International Business and Global Marketing. Electives range from 100 to 400 level and, in addition to what is listed below, topics courses on major issues are offered. (Please note that, as in all programs described in this chapter, changes are made from time to time.) Elective courses include the following:

World Class Operations
Management of Change
Asia: 1997
Americas: 1999
Africa: 2000
Europe in Change
Transnational (Global) Management
Introduction to Geography
International Relations
Political Philosophy
Public Administration and Policy
Third World Politics
Modern Political Systems: Europe
Recent U.S. History
Contemporary Europe
History of Russia, 1825 to Present
History of Modern China
History of Modern Japan
History of England
20th Century Diplomatic History
Beginning Japanese, I and II
Comparative Religion
Population
Beginning Spanish, I and II
Intermediate Spanish, I and II
Commercial Spanish

History, business, sociology, religion, languages, and so on may also be taken as electives. These courses are all designed to improve students' awareness of and appreciation for various cultures, including their own.

Graduate Programs

People who earn advanced degrees are highly valued, because of the in-depth nature of graduate studies. In short, people who complete graduate-level programs are more likely to be perceived as experts in their chosen fields.

Graduate school is very different from undergraduate studies, and I urge you to start by trying one course. Taking it a course at a time will let you get acclimated to graduate school and, even if your employer won't pay for an advanced degree, the company might be willing to pick up the tab for one or more courses that will help you do better in your present position and/or prepare for the next rung on the ladder.

A warning is in order here: Many students who have just completed their four-year degrees want to take a break. Unfortunately, for many the months very quickly turn into years, and they still have not started grad school. This is particularly inexcusable when your employer will pay for some, if not all, of a graduate degree program. In grad school, you get to delve more deeply into topics, as the following description of a class session at Webster University in St. Louis illustrates:

Dr. David Brennan's graduate-level marketing students at Webster University in Saint Louis come from many different places and represent a variety of age groups. Some are traditional university students who are going straight through to their MBAs before entering the work force full time. A number of students are from overseas and are enrolled in day classes as well. The majority are coming straight from work. The class meets for a four-hour session once a week for nine consecutive weeks and earns three credit hours.

There is a great deal of mutual respect in the class, and students make observations whenever they have something to contribute. This greatly enhances the learning experience, as the foreign students can discuss what does and does not work in their countries, and the students from the corporate world freely discuss their organizations' approaches.

The class is in international marketing and looks at foreign firms marketing in the United States as well as American companies attempting to penetrate overseas markets.

The first order of business is for students to discuss their term projects. Dr. Brennan and the other students provide suggestions to people who are encountering difficulties. There is a healthy give and take, and the atmosphere is very positive.

Next comes the first in-depth case study of the evening, involving the marketing of software in several different countries. Strategies are discussed in great detail, and Dave asks many penetrating questions. Critical concerns, such as the size of potential markets, competition, and even the configuration of software if it is to be produced in a language other than English show the students just how much thought, effort, and risk go into a decision to attempt to market overseas.

After a break, the topic changes to selling U.S. fast food overseas. The students watch a video on a U.S.-franchised fast-food company in Japan, and a lively discussion ensues as the foreign students talk about similar operations in their countries, and American students who have traveled abroad talk about their experiences in "American dining" overseas.

After another break, a detailed case study on the motorcycle industry occupies the class for the balance of the period. Cultures, lifestyles, production quotas, helmet laws, and advertising provide superb fodder for discussion.

The case studies involve high-tech, low-tech, and no-tech ventures and elicit in-depth analyses of how organizations in various industries and in many different countries handle their marketing mixes (product, promotion, distribution, and pricing).

In grad school, you are studying something you have chosen, and so is everyone else in the class. The concentrated program lets you delve more deeply into things that interest you, and the amount of useful knowledge you are able to glean in even a single class session is truly amazing. So, if there is any way you can go to graduate school, do.

A representative school, Babson College, in Babson Park (Wellesley) Massachusetts, offers a variety of MBA programs and an international management internship program. The college also offers an International Concentration for MBA candidates. Babson's language requirement should serve as a model for other schools: "All International Concentration candidates must demonstrate proficiency in a second language by graduation, as measured by the American Council on the Teaching of Foreign Languages, Advanced Level."[2]

Babson's programs require working on projects with mentor companies, as well as the standard academic load. Thus, graduates will have hands-on experience, which is greatly valued by employers.

Another representative program, Thunderbird, The American Graduate School of International Management, is also a strong supporter of internships and overseas programs. It offers language courses in Arabic, Chinese, French, German, Italian, Japanese, Portuguese, Russian, and Spanish, as well as English as a second language for foreign students. The Glendale, Arizona-based school is prominent in the field of international business training, and its emphasis on language training is well worth noting.

At the end of this chapter you will find a list of publications that will acquaint you with colleges and universities throughout the United States.

Foreign Schools

The information on the aforementioned American schools provides you with an overview of what your domestic competitors are doing. Now, let's look at what someone in another country who may be competing with you at some point is studying.

---

[2] 1994–95 Babson Graduate School of Business catalog, 57.

The European Business Management School is part of the University of Wales, Swansea. It offers degrees in the following areas:[3]

American Business Studies

Actuarial Studies

American Management Science

Business Studies

European Business Studies

European Management Science

Modern Languages with Business Studies

Management Science

Management Science and Mathematics

Management Science and Statistics

Operations Research

Statistics

The European Business Management School maintains exchange relationships with a number of universities in the United States and Canada, as well as in Austria, Belgium, Denmark, Finland, France, Germany, Greece, Hungary, The Netherlands, Portugal, Spain and Sweden.

Professor A. Diamantopoulos, the school's chair of international marketing, has a list of publications that runs fully 18 pages, and is working on yet another book as I write this. In short, although you may have never heard of the school until now, there, as in so many other places, you can be taught by professors with first-rate credentials. There are many truly fine schools—find the one that is right for you.

Someone I met in Israel a few years ago told me about his college days in the United States. He had wanted to study philosophy at a major school. His guidance counselor asked him, "As an undergraduate, which matters more to you, the professors or the name of the school on your degree?" The student replied, "I want to go to this school because of the professors." The guidance counselor told him about another school in the vicinity, where the professors from the famous school served as adjunct faculty. He said, "There, you'll be able to study with the same teachers, but the classes will be smaller and the tuition's a lot less." The student opted for the "lesser" school.

He received more personal attention, as the professors actually spent time with their students at the smaller school, while teaching assistants handled most of the student contact at the famous institution. When the time came for graduate studies, he had no trouble gaining admission to the famous school, because he was already well known to the faculty.

---

[3] University of Wales, Swansea 1994–1995 catalog, ii, vi.

Choosing your school is a major decision, and a lot of the questions you answered earlier concerning where you would like to live and work also apply to choosing where to go to school. The reference sources at the end of the chapter will help in this regard, and so will on-campus visits while the school is in session.

WHAT IF YOU HAVE "COMPLETED" YOUR EDUCATION?

While I am seeing an increasing number of people who are going after a second undergraduate degree in order to make themselves more employable and/or promotable, this is not an affordable (or even desirable) option for everyone. The critical thing is to take the honest assessment you have made of your education and experience in relation to what you want to do, and to work on overcoming your deficiencies.

Expertise is, as was mentioned earlier, vital in terms of making you appeal to prospective employers in the international sector. Along with that, you should follow Socrates' dictum and be "a citizen of the world."

Foreigners almost invariably have a better working knowledge of the world than do their American counterparts. That is why colleges and universities are upgrading their curricula to provide more relevant education for their students. As we discovered in Chapter 2, language training is always desirable, and it is frequently advisable to study more than one language at a time. This is particularly true if you plan to seek work in a country where more than one language is spoken. If you lack the funds to enter another multiyear academic program, you can take for-credit or noncredit language courses to make you a more promotable or a more desirable new hire.

The types of courses taught by the colleges and universities we looked at earlier will provide you with some excellent guidelines for further study. Language courses and conversation circles are particularly good and, in most areas, readily available.

It is frequently desirable to study more than one language at a time if possible. This is particularly true if the position you aspire to requires multiple fluencies.

Patricia Tarrant, an international banker in New York City, has an undergraduate degree in Romance Languages, and studied French, Italian and Spanish simultaneously. She said, "While I'd occasionally juxtapose a word, I found it very helpful to be studying three similar languages at the same time. Long term, it made me a better linguist, as I'd learned to appreciate the relationships among the three."

Ms. Tarrant urges securing a good working knowledge of grammar. She says, "Tapes are fine for giving you the 'feel' for a given language, and they also will provide you with some useful phrases. If you want to get beyond the superficial, however, you're going to have to learn the rules of grammar so that you can increase your ability to speak the language." She participates in conversation circles in order to stay current with her languages, and urges others to do the same.

ACTION PLAN

1. Begin addressing your educational needs by seeking information on various schools. Your reference librarian should be able to get you started, and many, if not all of the books on the following list should be readily available at your library:
   - *Cass & Birnbaum's Guide to American Colleges*
   - *The Fiske Guide to Colleges*
   - *The College Blue Book*
   - *Lovejoy's College Guide*
   - Peterson's Guides
     - *Two Year Colleges*
     - *Guide to Four Year Colleges*
     - *College Money Handbook*
     - *Competitive Colleges*
     - *Graduate and Professional Programs*
     - *Guide to American Graduate Schools* (Harold Doughty)
     - *The International Scholarship Book* (Daniel Cassidy)

   For information on careers:
   - *Occupational Handbook* (U.S. Dept. of Labor)

   For information on corporations:
   - *Million Dollar Directory* (Dun & Bradstreet)

2. Finally, if you have decided that you will need to move to another city to make yourself more employable, ask the reference librarian to direct you to a publications guide that will give you the names, addresses, and phone numbers of the daily papers in your target city. Call or write to the circulation department of one or more and arrange for a subscription.

   Reading the daily paper will teach you things that you will not find in a brochure from the Chamber of Commerce. Let's look at the paper, section by section:

- *International and national news:* How thoroughly do they cover these critical areas? Are there locally generated stories on a regular basis? If the answer is yes, it is a good sign in terms of local sophistication.
- *Business:* Once again, look for national and international stories and features (including syndicated ones) in addition to the usual local, state, and regional fare. How much awareness of international issues is displayed in this section?
- *Editorials:* Do the regular and guest editorials reflect an appreciation for the importance of international business in general, and increasing local participation in the international marketplace?

- *Real Estate Advertisements:* What is the housing market like compared to where you are living now? What do apartments rent for?
- *Employment Advertisements:* Who is hiring? Do they provide salary ranges in their ads?
- *Retail Advertising:* What do the items you normally purchase cost in this city?
- *Community Calendar:* What sort of activities that you enjoy take place regularly?
- *Letters to the Editors:* Do the writers address news topics as well as sports?

All of the above will provide you with an overview of what life is really like in your target city. That way, you will not be going in blind to its short-comings, and you will also have a much better feel for the good elements of life in that locale.

The information a newspaper can provide you is very valuable. Make the small investment it requires!

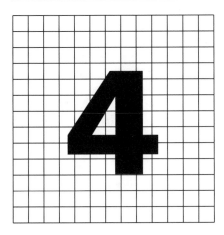

CAREERS IN SALES AND MARKETING

CHAPTER OBJECTIVES
Upon completion of this chapter, you should be able to:
1. Understand what sales and marketing positions are and are not
2. Assess your interest in these fields
3. Evaluate your qualifications
4. Prepare a plan for acquiring the tools you will need to pursue a sales and/or marketing career

SALES CAREERS

"Sales" is not a dirty word! Frequently, positions advertised under the heading of "Marketing" in the classifieds are actually sales positions. A person's business card may read "Marketing Representative," but if that person is not *selling,* he or she will not be employed for long.

Sales has had a negative connotation for many years, and we still laugh at archetypes like the door-to-door sales reps who plague Dagwood and other comic strip characters. These "salesmen" are pushing worthless products, literally stick a foot in the door, and will not take no for an answer.

In reality, today's salespeople are not this colorful. They are professionals whose main task is to help their customers.

What Salespeople Do

The bulk of selling, outside of telemarketing and retailing, is performed on a business-to-business basis. Men and women who succeed in this profession are, first of all, good listeners.

Listening is key to the selling process, because your prospective customers will, if you let them, tell you what you need to know to clinch the deal.

Let's start at the beginning. A *prospect* is someone who has a potential need for your product and also has the funds to pay for it (through his or her company) and the authority to make the buying decision. *Cold calling* is contacting a prospect and scheduling an appointment for presentation.

Your employer will have a list of prospective customers, but you are also expected to develop additional business, which means doing some prospecting on your own, particularly at trade shows and conventions.

In business-to-business selling, it is fairly easy to secure an appointment. There are a number of reasons for this. The first is that part of your prospect's job is to keep current with state-of-the-art products and services that are designed to help his or her organization do a better job. Second, it is helpful to prospects to know the representative for an alternative source and, finally, even if they are completely happy with their present vendor, it doesn't hurt for them to let their regular representative know that they have been talking with you. That way, they ensure that they will not be taken for granted by their current vendors.

Once you have the appointment, it is time to prepare for it. Your homework begins with learning everything you can about the prospect's organization. Have they purchased from your firm in the past? If so, what led to losing their business? Do they currently purchase from another division of your firm? If so, how is that relationship going?

What are their future plans? A look at their annual report is most helpful in this regard, as are industry and function specific publications, which keep you abreast of changing trends.

Which of your products lend themselves to this prospect's needs? Once you have determined this, bone up on the critical features of the products, with an emphasis on the specific benefits they will provide to this particular customer.

Be aware of the prospect's product and shopping alternatives. In short, know and respect your competitors. After all, they have market share, which means they are doing some things right!

It does not pay to criticize your competitors, because they are in the same business you are; so tearing them down is, by extension, putting your own organization down.

When you are selling internationally, either in the United States or overseas, a legitimate question a prospective client may ask is how you intend to service their account. What will you do if something goes wrong? Anticipate this question, because the answer to it may determine whether your sales proposal will even be considered.

If you are a contract representative for one or more firms, you should already have determined how much business you can legitimately handle. This is a valid concern for the firms you represent as well as for prospective customers because if you are spread too thin your efforts will be insufficient.

Years ago, Victor Kiam of Remington looked at sales in the Japanese market. At that point, his company was represented in Japan by a firm whose salespeople serviced a variety of accounts in addition to Remington's. Mr. Kiam arranged for a small sales organization to come into being in Japan, one that would devote all of its efforts to selling his firm's products. Not surprisingly, there was a very significant increase in sales.

Keep in mind that what you are selling—provided that your firm's products can meet your prospect's needs—is, very often, yourself. Sales reps work with their customers and help to facilitate the manufacturing and distribution processes in order to meet the customers' needs and deadlines.

Salespeople also help in the new product development process because they report what the competition is doing and relay customers' desires for new products.

If you are a conscientious problem solver and know what you are selling and its best applications, chances are that you will be able to overcome resistance, particularly when it comes to price, and get the order. As a salesperson you work with the customer, and provide value-added service (above and beyond the products itself) that can result in a cost justification even if your company charges more for its product.

Before a sales call, look at every possible objection a prospective customer may raise, and have satisfactory answers prepared in advance.

Your firm may have a canned presentation prepared, and may not allow significant deviations from the script. In the international realm, however, this is not likely, because cultural and linguistic differences come into play. In any event, plan your sequence of presentation in advance.

An old-timer once told me to be sure that I read the local paper each morning before I went out on calls. He said, "That way, you'll know what's going on that's of importance in the prospect's life, and you'll have some good opening conversational gambits."

In the international sector, it is of particular importance to know what can and cannot be discussed with someone from a given culture. Be very careful which topics you choose and, to play it safe, do not use humor, as many jokes do not transfer well to international settings. There may be a bit of small talk while you are settling in. Be pleasant, but not overly familiar.

Overcoming objections is something you will do a lot of during a sales call. The two most common objections are that the prospect's organization does not have the money to pay for your product and that it is too expensive anyway.

If what you are offering is going to help them do a better job, the money can be located somewhere in the organization. And, if you are truly a value-added representative, you are giving additional service value, so the perceived cost goes down.

Keep in mind that you will be tested frequently by prospects. They want to know that you are going to be there for the long haul. This is particularly true in the international sector.

In the old days, sales executives would say, "Don't take 'no' for an answer!" They would also complain if you "left money on the table," which means that you did not sell everything you could have.

Today, it is understood that there are legitimate reasons for saying no, and that rather than overselling now and losing the customer forever, you build gradually and develop an ongoing relationship which, in the long term, makes a lot more money for your organization.

Legitimate reasons for saying no include the following:

1. They really don't have the money now, because they have been told to hold the line on expenses.

2. They have recently purchased something similar from the competition, and it would be impolitic to try to replace it now.

3. They have no history with you and your firm, and so they have no idea about your staying power.

4. A major change in the firm's composition is pending (merger, takeover, and so on), and their people have been told to refrain from purchasing anything new so that the firm can cut short-term costs, thereby maximizing profits.

A sales manager I did some consulting for recently told me, "We want to penetrate new markets. I've told our reps to contact prospects regularly, even though they aren't ordering from us. Over a period of time, it will occur to them that they hear from us more often than they do the people they're buying from. In other words, our competitor's taking them for granted. At that point, we'll start doing business."

As we've seen elsewhere, long-term relationships are the norm in the international sector, so persistence is definitely a virtue!

The *close* is something that happens again and again in a sales call. Ironically, your first close will come very early on in your presentation when you state why you are there.

After an objection has been raised and you have satisfied the prospect with your answer, close again. Do this each time you handle an objection. Finally, at the end of the presentation, *Ask for the order!* That is, after all, why you are there.

Follow up with calls and letters as appropriate. Personalize them to the greatest extent possible, but within culturally acceptable boundaries. If the prospect is interested in a particular activity, and you see an article on it in a newspaper or magazine, cut it out and send it along with a note. This helps to solidify the fact that you see prospects as individuals and appreciate them for who they are. It opens a lot of doors, and makes the business relationship a lot more pleasant.

Travel sounds glamorous until you have done it for a while. Trade shows, conventions, and traveling take up a lot of time and cut into your personal life.

To begin with, you will probably need to develop a way to skip one meal a day, replacing it with a small portion of fruit and/or juice. The reason for this is that meals are very often a key part of the sales process, and if you are skimping on yourself, you are basically telling the person you are entertaining to go lightly, too. Generally, that does not sit very well. If at all possible, try not to schedule three business meals on any one day. This will provide you with at least one private opportunity to cut back on your caloric intake. (More on this later.)

While we are on the subject of food, be open to new dining experiences. It is fun, educational, and just plain good business. Developing a taste for international cuisines is a must if you want to deal with foreign entities.

Compensation

Compensation for sales representatives varies, as does the method of payment. For example, some firms pay on a straight commission basis. This scares a lot of people, who ask, "But what if I don't sell anything?" The answer to that is, if you don't sell anything, your compensation is a moot point, because you won't be working there for very long.

Good sales reps prefer commissions, because it makes the amount of money they make a product of their own initiative, rather than settling for a fixed amount. If you have something in reserve to support you while you are establishing yourself in a sales career, commissions can wait. Generally, people who are embarking upon a second career and who are receiving a pension (for example, retired military, teachers), can handle the start-up phase long enough to determine if they are cut out for sales.

Some firms will pay a draw against future commissions, and others will provide a stipend for a short period while you are getting on your feet.

Salaries plus commission is another compensation possibility, but this is generally for positions that require a long gestation period for the order to be placed. During that time, you will be working extensively with the customers, helping to shape the right combination of products and services to meet their needs. Selling oil field supplies is a good example of this because, even on the same patch, every hole is different.

There are also variations of the foregoing, such as straight salary or salary with bonuses. The critical question before accepting any sales job is, are you financially secure enough to give you an honest chance of succeeding on the job?

Characteristics of Successful Salespeople

Good salespeople bounce back from hearing negative responses, because they do not take the rejections (and there are a lot of them) personally. They learn from each encounter, reshape their presentations, and keep on plugging.

The real pros are not desperate. They are willing to take whatever time it takes to eventually win a prospect over. Desperation shows! If you are up against it, and your career's on the line, your nonverbal communication will be a dead giveaway, and the prospect will back off.

Professionals do not oversell. Their main function is to help the customer determine needs, and to match products and services so that the needs are satisfied. Through sheer force of personality you may be able to sell someone something they don't really need. This will provide short-term gain for you, but it is an example of winning the battle but losing the war. Customers will quickly come to resent what you did, and new orders will be a long time coming, if indeed they ever do business with you again.

Business-to-business selling is a profession. Unlike part-time sales, such as real estate, where "dabblers" may sell several houses a year and let it go at that, in business-to-business selling, you are going to be on call all the time. There is a great deal of pressure to produce, because there are plenty of people who want your job.

Solid professionals are not frightened by competition, they welcome it. Can *you* handle this pressure?

A sales job is not for everyone, and the fact that you have sold one thing in a given industry does not mean that you can sell all things. Each sales situation is somewhat different, and that is even more the case in international sales, either here or abroad.

Preparing To Enter a Career in Sales

The place to start in sales is with a domestic sales position, one that will enable you to gain experience and assess your potential for any sales career, whether domestic or international.

Your best bet is to save money from your present job (not a bad plan in any case) and wait until you have got a minimum of six months, basic expenses in the bank. This includes the following:

- Rent or mortgage payments
- Car payments, insurance, gas and oil, and maintenance fees
- Clothing allowance
- Health and life insurance (Be prepared to pay for your own benefits if the sales job does not work out and you become unemployed. Also, budget for disability insurance.)
- Food
- Entertainment (This is vital. You will need to get away from the pressures of the new job.)
- Other: child support, contingency budget, and so on.

Better yet, bank a year or more of basic expenses before seeking a sales job, because it will make you that much more secure, and you will end up giving yourself a better chance of succeeding.

I realize that it can take a long time to bank what you need, but if you are contemplating a new career, consider this savings plan to be an investment in your long-term future.

Also, as you begin to derive income from sales, replenish your basic expenses savings account. This will help you to take a less desperate, more professional approach to your sales job, which will lead to your making more money.

As you begin to close in on your savings goals, start checking the classifieds for sales positions. Do not accept one prematurely. In sales, the "opportunity of a lifetime" actually is always there for the taking, because there is a tremendous amount of turnover in entry-level sales positions. This is because most new salespeople cannot make enough to pay for their basic expenses while they are attempting to establish themselves in sales. Happily, this will not be *your* problem if you build up your savings first.

Thanks to your banking the necessary money to carry on with your present lifestyle for a protracted period, you will be more secure when it comes to looking for that first sales job, and you will not have to take the first one that comes along.

Consider using an employment agency, in addition to or instead of answering classified ads. The agency representatives, once they know what you are looking for, can set up worthwhile interviews for you. In order to do this, you will need to answer the following questions:

1. What types of products and/or services would you feel comfortable selling?

2. Are you willing to travel? If so, how far and how often?

3. Are you willing to relocate? If so, immediately, or after a training period that helps you to determine if you're comfortable with the company and the job?

   Also, if relocation is an acceptable option, are you prepared to make the move? How about your lease or mortgage? What about your personal life, including your significant others?

   Does the company pay relocation expenses? Will it help you to pay off your lease or sell your home? If you require this sort of assurance up front, tell the agency. That way, they will not send you to a firm that does not meet your needs.

4. Are you willing to pay part or all of the employment fee for the job? Please note that a lot of firms will be willing to reimburse you for at least a portion of the fee, if you work out, and many companies will pay the fee themselves. The important issue here is if you are not willing to pay any fee, ever, let them know up front. That way, you are not wasting anyone's time, because you will not be interviewed for those jobs.

Qualifications Needed for Sales Positions

Some sales positions have very specific requirements, including a particular degree. Obviously, if you are in the technical realm, this is understandable.

Other types of sales careers are open to people with general backgrounds, and a degree may be desirable, but not necessary.

Here are some areas of study that are helpful (the courses do not have to be taken for college credit):

Marketing
Psychology
Public speaking
Communications: interpersonal and small group
Languages

It goes without saying that you need to like to and be able to work with people in all kinds of settings in order to succeed in sales. This includes one-on-one and both small and large groups.

This does not mean that you have to be a "back-slapper." What is most important is that you know who you are, and that you are consistent in your approach. Here are three examples of sales reps whom I have worked with. Each has a very different personality.

"A" is the brash, know-it-all, kid-brother type. He comes on strong as a problem solver. People don't necessarily like him, but they respect his intelligence and his work ethic. He never goes in unprepared, and he is a good listener, so that he is able to gather additional information in order to help solve his customers' problems.

"B" majored in history. Like "A," she is always well prepared in terms of her prospect firms' histories and needs. She is also a good listener. She is fascinating to be with on a sales call, because she manages to work world history into her presentations, and the customers feel like King John signing the Magna Charta as they execute their purchase orders.

"C" is another good listener. (This is an important quality in salespeople.) He was too small to play college football, so of course he played varsity all four years. He was also too small for the pros, but he managed to squeeze out a couple of years there, too. He is a driven individual, and very intense. He is also quite flashy in his dress and the vehicles he drives. His customers don't resent this, because he has the ability to carry it off, and is enjoying himself, not lording it over us lesser mortals. In fact, he is so happy, you are happy for him.

All three of these salespeople do not oversell. That is, they do not try to get customers to buy something they do not really need. As a result, they get repeat business.

Two of them are genuinely likeable, and "A" is so good at what he does, people are eager to work with him, anyway, because he is helping them. And that is crucial. Again and again, I have seen cost justifications written for higher-ticket items because the salesperson is working with and for the customer.

Travel

Most domestic sales positions require travel. Even if your territory is a major metropolitan area, you can still count on a fair amount of travel to sales meetings, trade shows, and conventions.

If you cover a large territory, you will spend a lot of your time behind the wheel of a company car and/or a rental. You will also do a lot of flying.

All of this sounds very glamorous, but you need to be aware of the fact that you are going to have to spend a great deal of time away from home on most sales jobs and, once you have entered the international arena, even if you are based in the United States, you are going to be on the road more than ever.

Let me give you a look at a typical three-day trade show schedule.

Sunday: 8:00 a.m., fly from Denver to the show's city, arriving at 1:00 p.m., local time. Pick up rental car, and drive to hotel. Check in and make certain that my shipment of flyers has arrived from the home office. They are being held for me in the baggage room, which is an improvement over my previous trip, when the printer was late and I had to carry four boxes of flyers, with a total weight of 160 pounds, as "checked luggage."

My hotel is nearly an hour from the site of the trade show, as the firm I am representing was a late entry, and the hotels that are nearby were booked solid very early.

I load the flyers into my car and head downtown to the hotel where we were able to book a hospitality suite. Once there, one of the salespeople meets me and we carry the boxes to the hotel's baggage room ourselves, as the bellmen are swamped and we have a meeting to get to.

There has been no time for lunch, so I grab a can of juice on my way into the meeting with the regional manager and her staff. She has been in town for two days, and the booth has been set up. She goes over our schedules for the show, which begins tomorrow morning at eight. It turns out that our chief competitor is coming out with a major new product, and that we have next to no information about it. Everyone reports on what they have heard, and now it is time to open up the hospitality suite to welcome existing and prospective customers.

The hotel has outdone itself, but I only nibble at the hors d'oeuvres, for two reasons: first, another salesperson and I are taking two customers to dinner and, second, you are always "on" at one of these gatherings, and carrying food and making sure there is nothing stuck in your teeth is too much to worry about when you should be conversing with customers on behalf of the firm.

I sip at a glass of club soda with lime, so it looks as though I am having an alcoholic beverage, and I "work" the room.

Dinner starts with drinks at the restaurant, and I really nurse a gin and tonic. I also choose food that is easy to eat, so that I am free to continue working. Happily, I am hungry, so I am not concerned about caloric intake.

After dinner, we go back to the hospitality suite, and the event continues until shortly after midnight. Awash with club soda, I drive back and enjoy a hearty four hours of sleep, as I have to get up early and meet four customers at their hotel for a quick breakfast. I am going to be there mostly as window dressing, because the sales rep who handles their territory is going to be carrying the conversational ball most of the time.

By 7:30, I am in our booth, setting things up for the day's activities. I have another dinner scheduled for tonight, so I arrange to skip lunch by the simple expedient of agreeing to continue working the booth after downing a quick can of juice. Working the booth entails being on your feet—and, figuratively speaking, your toes—all day. With the exception of an occasional restroom break and an hour spent checking out the rest of the show, especially our competition's offerings, I am in the booth until the close of exhibit hours at 6 p.m. After that, there is dinner with the customers and more time in the hospitality suite.

The second day of the show, and my third in town, follow pretty much the same script, except that I have both lunch and dinner with customers. This is tricky, because I prefer to eat a rather large breakfast. Today, however, I have some toast, juice, and an apple, followed by a brief walk. Then I go back to the booth and, after dinner, take another shift in the hospitality suite.

Once again, as day four of the three-day show begins, I am facing the world on four hours of sleep. Today, there is another breakfast with customers, followed by five hours in the booth. Then, it is time to help disassemble the booth and prepare it for shipment to another site. I have juice for lunch, as there is one more dinner to be worked, and I am in the hospitality suite until it is time to leave for the restaurant. After the meal, I have the rest of the evening off.

I take a walk around the downtown area and get to see something of the city for the first time during the four days I have been there. I also get a good night's sleep. The next morning, I am able to use my hotel's pool for the first and last time during my stay, and I have nearly one and a half hours to myself before I move on to the next city. That afternoon I arrive at the next site and help to set up our alternate booth (the one I helped to dismantle and pack yesterday is en route to another location, and I will be reunited with it in a few days), and then hustle off to dinner with several customers.

This particular trip saw me out of town for 22 straight days as, in addition to shows and conventions, I had to spend 4 days at a customer's place of business, helping to straighten out a problem with one of our products.

During that time, I stole whatever time I could, to try to see something of the places I was visiting, but it required a great deal of effort to get away, even for an hour or so.

Although I did get to do some "recreational" things with customers, such as attend a concert or a baseball game, keep in mind that I had to be "on" the entire time, as I was still serving as an ambassador for my company.

At that point in my career, I was averaging three weeks out of every four on the road, but I was allowed home for "weekends" whenever possible. This consisted of arriving in Denver on Friday night and heading back out to the airport on Sunday, so I would be ready for the next show or sales call.

I got to visit a lot of truly glamorous places, but these were working trips, and I frequently saw only the airport, hotel, and meeting site.

My first trip to British Columbia, for example, lasted all of six hours. I flew in from Winnipeg that morning, spent several hours (including lunch) conducting market research, and flew on to the next city that afternoon.

I am not telling you this to denigrate the travel aspects of sales and marketing positions. I was well paid and, for a while, I truly enjoyed the hotels and the jets, but there really is a point where the glamour vanishes.

Sales is not for everyone. You are expected to perform consistently, and a lot of people simply are not up to the pressure. It is difficult enough to handle the job domestically, but international positions, even when you are based in your own country, are more demanding, because you have to operate within two cultures: your own, and that of the country where your employer is located.

International sales is even more complicated if you are based or traveling overseas, living and working in a foreign culture. This is interesting and exciting, but it is not easy.

Sales jobs are always available because the neophyte failure rate is so high, and even old hands burn out eventually. The pressure is unrelenting because every year the quota (probably expanded) needs to be met again.

Most salespeople spend a great deal of time on their own, which has certain pluses, but also means that your social support system will be skeletal at best.

If you are involved in international selling, your territory, whether in the United States or abroad, is likely to be huge, and covering it will require extended periods of time away from home. It will also put considerable strain on you physically (jet lag, digestive problems, for example), mentally (keeping cultural nuances straight while making your presentations and so on), and emotionally (dealing with personal problems while you are away from the people who matter most to you).

You will also miss a lot of things you may currently take for granted, such as children's birthday parties, dance recitals, soccer games, and so on.

A salesperson once called me at the office. The call was forwarded to our customer service department, where I was attending a surprise birthday party for one of our phone reps. I answered the salesperson's business question, and then he asked, "What's all the laughing about in the background?" I explained that we were celebrating a birthday and, after a long pause, he said wistfully, "That sounds like fun. You know, with my travel schedule the way it is, I haven't been home for any family birthdays, including my own, for years."

Be sure to take into account the negative aspects along with all of the positive ones when you consider a career in sales.

MARKETING CAREERS

Let's turn now to marketing. There are three wide-open areas for Americans to work for international firms right here in the United States: public relations, specialty advertising, and market research. Let's look at them one at a time. In each case, it is wise to test yourself in the domestic marketplace before looking for international work.

Public Relations

Public relations is an often-misunderstood profession. I recall working for a firm that had not been in the business press for several years prior to my signing a part-time consulting agreement with them. Like any company that had let things slip in the area, there was a backlog of newsworthy stories to get out.

For several months, I was able to send editors and columnists useful items, and, every week, the company was mentioned at least once, and frequently two or three times in various publications. During this period, in the eyes of the CEO, I could do no wrong, and my 30-day contracts were lovingly renewed.

The company received local, regional, national, and, on a few noteworthy occasions, even international notice. Then, for several weeks, there was nothing at all. During that period, I set up a long article with a major publication, one that would be published two months hence. I also sent releases to major quarterlies and fielded questions from their editors, and was assured that coverage would ensue.

At the end of the month my contract was not renewed, because the CEO had not "seen our name in the paper in *weeks*!" I attempted to explain about the upcoming stories, that, in the absence of new products, great sales results, charitable contributions, and significant new hires, we were not going to get into the daily press, and that my efforts were directed toward getting mentions in major trade publications—the ones our *customers* read. His reply was, "That's not good enough. The fact is, after a flashy start, you're not giving us enough bang for the buck!"

I wasn't replaced and, for the next several months, they were mentioned in the quarterlies and, of course, the major article appeared. Then, for nearly a year, there was nothing. At that point, he hired a full-time PR specialist, and having learned a lesson, the CEO stepped back and let her do her work.

"PR types" have traditionally been eyed askance by executives. Dubbed "spin doctors," until recently, they were called in to "fix" things when an organization had made "bad" news.

We have entered the era of *integrated marketing,* and now, more and more, the PR people are in at the very beginning, along with advertising and marketing personnel. Finally, PR professionals are in a position to advise their employers *before* plans are carried out.

PR specialists are responsible for promoting their clients in the media. News stories generally have a more favorable impact on the marketplace than advertisements do because news items have an ascribed credibility, while ads are usually suspect.

Editors, reporters, and columnists are always on the lookout for newsworthy stories. "Newsworthy" generally means the type of stories the medium runs regularly.

Reading a wide variety of publications that pertain to a client's industry will teach you a great deal about some very important things:

1. What types of stories get published in the trade press?
2. What is being said about the competition?
3. What are the publications' and columnists' "voices" like?

Let's go through these points one at a time.

Types of stories.   It is useless to send a publication a story that does not meet the editorial guidelines. First of all, when you have identified a target for an article, familiarize yourself with the contents of several issues. Then, check the masthead, and contact the appropriate editor for a formal set of guidelines. Generally speaking, trade publications are receptive to articles from within the industry. Occasionally, if a good story idea is really good, they may assign one of their own people to write it. In that case, your task is to facilitate the writer's access to key people in your company.

Usually, though, the publications prefer an article written by someone from the firm you are representing. If there is a good writer on staff, and he or she has the time *and* the title to pen a credible article, you will function as an in-house editor and also gather whatever information the writer needs to complete the task.

Frequently, though, you will write the article yourself for someone else's byline. If "ghosting" is beneath you, consider another line of work.

You should meet as often as possible with the person you are writing for, to coordinate the flow of information and to master the use of his or her "voice." (We will deal with "voices" later on.) The more you work with the person, the better the story is likely to be, and the more secure the person will feel about lending his or her name to it. Finally, good stories tend to be followed up. Making your "writer" thoroughly conversant with what is going out under his or her name will make for better interviews down the road.

Occasionally, you may need to provide more than one "voice." On one of my early ghosting assignments, I told the person who had hired me that the story, which was ostensibly written by a senior vice president, needed only a snappy quote from the president to be complete. My boss asked me to provide something useful, and so I did. When the article appeared in print, the president sent me a note, saying, "Good article...and I loved the snappy quote!"

Here is one more story about ghosting, from a woman who is in charge of corporate communications for a very large firm: One day, a press release she had written was printed intact in three different papers. In every instance, the byline was that of a business reporter for the publication. She did not complain, because those names gave the release an enormous amount of credibility.

What is being said about the competition?   If you have been hired to PR for a firm, chances are that their competitors have been receiving lots of coverage. It is counterproductive to criticize the competition because they are, after all, in the same industry as your client, and you want to be as positive as you can about the industry itself. Remember, the competition has customers, so they must be doing *something* right.

Your stories should deal with differences that make a difference. Provide a unique angle (and, if you have been reading the trade press faithfully, you will know what hasn't been covered yet) that positions your client as something of an innovator.

What are the publications' and columnists' "voices" like?   Back in the sixties, when I was a student at the Defense Information School, one of the courses I took was writing for TV and radio. Our instructor, a crusty old Army officer, would give us an assignment and a five- or ten-minute deadline. He would then pace up and down, informing us every 15 seconds or so how little time we had left and, again and again, he would exhort us to "Write like you talk!"

Under those circumstances, we were forced to simplify. I would pretend that I was sending a telegram at $50 a word, and try to complete the assignment in as few words as possible. Economizing led to success, because the stuff I wrote was easy to understand.

When someone reads something you have written, they should "hear" your voice throughout the communication. Too often, though, when we start to write something, we become stilted in an attempt to be formal or sound learned. This interrupts the flow of the narrative and reduces the impact of the message.[1]

Voice is also important when you are tailoring a release for a specific column. If you are able to match the publication's style, you are much more likely to get the release printed intact, and thanks to computers and word processors, this is easy to do.

For example, if you have written a one- or two-page general circulation release on a new product and you want to be certain that it gets mentioned in a specific column, send a separate release written in the column's format to the editor or columnist. Suppose that news blurbs in the column don't run any more than five lines. If you have written your general release in the standard style, putting the "Who, what, when, and where" in your first paragraph, it will be easy for you to encapsulate the news release in a few lines for the column.

That first paragraph corresponds to the "Executive Summary" discussed in the section on writing business plans—it is a brief overview of the entire story. The format has been around for years, simply because it works. Most news stories are written in the "inverted pyramid" style, with the tightly written overview coming first and the rest of the story giving supplemental information. This is done so that if an ad comes in at the last moment, the story can be cut at the end of any paragraph, and the advertisement can be inserted.

This format is also helpful in broadcasting. Newscasters read at varying rates of speed. The average is around 17 lines of copy per minute. News stories from the wire services tend to have more than one paragraph. The first paragraph provides the overview. If the newscaster is running slow and wants to get all of the stories in, he or she can simply read the first paragraph, ad lib a transition, and move on to the first paragraph of the next story. When the newscaster runs out of copy, he or she can say, "Reviewing the top story of the hour..." and go back and read as many paragraphs of that story as needed to fill in the time. The point of all this is that, once past the overview, the rest of the release is expendable.

---

[1] John Tarrant's *Business Writing With Style* (New York: John Wiley & Sons, 1991) is a good primer for business communicators.

Now that we have looked into some of the things PR people do, how do you get into the field when no one is hiring and, even if they were, you don't have any experience? Here is how one person did it:

Maxine Whidden (not her real name) is a very successful PR practitioner. A number of years ago, when the last of her children was finishing school, Maxine decided that she might like to get into advertising and public relations.

She had graduated from college with a degree in English more than 25 years ago, and had gotten married shortly after graduation. She had never been in the work force, and had no experience in the field.

Several of Maxine's friends were in the profession, and she briefly toyed with the idea of having one of them pull a few strings and land her an entry-level position. Happily, it occurred to her that that was not a good idea.

What if a friend did manage to get her hired instead of other qualified people and then, after vaulting over the other applicants, she decided that she really didn't want to be in the field after all? If she then left, her friend would look bad at work, and the friendship would be severely strained.

It suddenly occurred to her that there was a place that needed help—the publicity committee of the small symphony she belonged to. Like the other musicians, she had grumbled when attendance was low because the publicity committee had failed to get the news of the concert out in time for free exposure, but she had never wanted to become involved with the publicity because she was playing in the orchestra for fun, and serving on a committee was too much like work!

Now that she was looking for work, though, the committee looked pretty good. At the next rehearsal, she volunteered and, within a few minutes, she had been named committee chair, because her predecessor was tired of the "thankless" task.

It occurred to Maxine that the mechanics of the whole thing were quite simple:

1. Identify the target publications and broadcast media.
2. Notify them in a timely manner.

Her predecessor had done a good job of identifying the targets. They were:

1. A classical FM station
2. Two AM talk stations
3. An NPR affiliate station
4. Three network television affiliates
5. A local cable television station
6. Two local independent television stations
7. A PBS affiliate station
8. The daily newspaper
9. Two monthly magazines

10.   One alternative weekly newspaper

11.   A monthly arts calendar newsletter

The list was pretty thorough, but Maxine decided to add music teachers from the school system to it, along with the newspaper at a nearby college. She selected the latter because several faculty members played in the orchestra, but their only contribution to publicizing the group was to put up a poster on a community bulletin board.

Her predecessor's biggest failing lay in the area of contacting targets on time and in a relevant format. Maxine set out to change things.

The orchestra's concerts qualified for mention on the air and in print. Maxine met with the right people at each target organization and found out what format they wanted their releases in and when they needed to receive them in order to make their deadlines.

The publicity committee had, in addition to being late, frequently failed to list all of the basics (who, what, when, and where) and a phone number to be called for more information. Maxine included this information and began preparing her releases in the desired formats. She also met her deadlines.

For the first time in years, a concert was promoted by all of the target media. This, combined with hard work by the poster committee, led to a sold-out performance.

The next step was for Maxine to produce her first radio public service announcement (PSA). PSAs are the bane of an announcer's existence. It is amazing just how many PSAs have not been properly prepared for recording by spelling out the basics. Frequently, dates and times are omitted from PSA copy that has been prepared by publicity committee members. All too often though, there is no information number, and so the free announcement is discarded and the announcer simply goes on to the next one. The publicity committee, having met their delivery deadline, decides to stop sending releases to the station because the announcement was not aired.

Maxine cranked out copy that could be read or recorded the moment it arrived at the station. She also worked at cultivating contacts and, in the process, learned that there were set times of the day and night when PSAs were being recorded. This gave her the idea to start producing her own recorded spots.

Several professional actors had been used by the orchestra to do narrations during certain performances. Maxine was able to persuade them to contribute talent in the form of taping PSAs for the orchestra.

The actors, who were well known locally, would go to a radio station with Maxine when a regular announcer was cranking out PSAs. The announcer was happy to take a break while Maxine and an engineer had the actor record a PSA or two. The actor would identify himself, give the group a plug, and leave. Maxine would then ask the engineer to run several dubs. These were taken to other stations as finished PSAs, and the original would be used on the air by the recording station.

Maxine seldom had to pay for the dubs, but when she did, the charges were minimal. She always had one extra dub made "for the archives" (her portfolio).

The dubs also ran well on television as sound underneath a community calendar slide or a picture of the orchestra.

Maxine also did not neglect the print media. She carefully cultivated contacts at newspapers and magazines and arranged for several articles to be written about the orchestra and its ambitious concert schedule. Maxine added copies of the articles to her portfolio.

The articles led to her being able to arrange television and radio interviews featuring the conductor and various key musicians. Some of the television interviews featured clips from rehearsals and performances, so everyone in the group received additional exposure. Maxine added video and audio tapes of the interviews to her portfolio.

Meanwhile, the orchestra continued to play to sold-out houses.

At the end of her second year as the orchestra's PR person, Maxine decided that it was time to produce a television PSA. She arranged with a production house in her area to produce a PSA—after midnight on a weeknight—without charge.

Maxine managed to assemble the entire orchestra in the studio to perform while the cameras rolled. The television stations were delighted to run the spot, and, once again, the concert was sold out.

Maxine had given herself two years to "try marketing." By now, she had decided that she liked it, and most important of all, she knew what it was all about.

Because she had a full portfolio, she was now ready to approach employers.

She had a friend at an ad agency where an entry-level job was available. The friend arranged for an interview. Maxine dazzled them with her portfolio and her references—key people at television and radio stations, newspapers, and magazines—and got the job. Today, she runs her own agency.

You might say, "Well, wasn't she lucky that she had a friend who was able to get her the interview!" I am tempted to quote the late Branch Rickey, who said, "Luck is the residue of design."

The fact is, Maxine had prepared herself for the world of work. And, in the process, she was also able to help a group whose philosophy and goals she valued.

She was also fortunate to reside in a large city, with its heavy concentration of media. Perhaps your home town does not offer this scope, and you are planning to move to a city where you don't know anyone. One of the best ways to establish yourself in a new locale is to join a group of kindred spirits.

It could be a religious organization, theater group, chorale, and so on. Choose a group that you will enjoy, and the publicity committee will almost certainly welcome you with open arms. Thus, Maxine's blueprint can be adapted to meet your needs.

In fact, the odds are that you don't even have to move to try your modified version of her plan. Even very small communities have churches, glee clubs, folk dancing groups, and so on, so you can put her plan into action just about anywhere. Once you have proven yourself as a PR person for the group, you are in a position to solicit business from members of the group who run their own businesses. In fact, if Maxine had not gotten the job with the agency, that is precisely what she would have done.

Finally, what if, after two years of hard, unpaid work, Maxine had decided that she didn't want a marketing career? She says, "If I'd decided to do something else, I'd have had no regrets. After all, I got to try things out, without making a commitment or putting a friend's reputation with their firm on the line. I'd know for a fact just *why* I didn't like marketing, so I'd be in a position to make a well-informed decision about my career. Lastly, for two years I made significant contributions, beyond my playing, to a group I loved. That in itself was worth the effort."

Maxine moved to another city years ago, but her former orchestra continues to do what she did, and they are thriving.

Chances are, you already belong to a group that is as important to you as the orchestra was to Maxine. Or, you may have identified such a group. Either way, they are waiting for you!

Specialty Advertising   Chances are, you are wearing, carrying, or using something produced by the specialty advertising industry. It may be a sweatshirt, coffee mug, calendar, key chain, or one of thousands of other items that carry a corporate or organizational logo and/or advertising message.

These items are frequently used as giveaways after sales presentations or at trade shows and conventions. They may also be premiums, which you receive when you purchase a product, such as a lighter attached to a carton of cigarettes.

The goal of the specialty advertiser is to provide you with something that you will use, look at (and have others who come into your orbit see it, too), and eventually, heed the message.

Ray Morgan is prominent in this industry, and he is constantly coming up with new items for his customers. The challenge is to provide something that will exert a positive influence on everyone who comes in contact with it. Having done that once, you are expected to keep coming up with new ideas, so the pressure is really on, as there is a lot of competition in this field.

Of course, there are also a lot of opportunities, and you are most likely going to break in as a commission-only rep. This is something that you can try on your own, either on a part-time basis or on behalf of an organization you belong to.

For example, years ago, Ray helped a church increase its Sunday attendance by having "Let God Straighten Out Your Life" printed on a pencil that looked like a pretzel. Along with the snappy one-liner was the church's name, address, and times of services. This was used as a giveaway to potential parishioners, and it achieved the desired effect.

Certain items could be used as fund raisers, and by coordinating this with a specialty advertising firm, you can test the waters and see if you would like to do this sort of thing. Specialty advertising is a hybrid field, as it involves both sales and marketing skills, and it is no place for the timid, as the market is highly competitive.

Ray advocates continuing to study marketing. He reads textbooks, attends lectures, and audits courses. He says, "The day that I think I've learned all there is to know about marketing is the day I'm on my way out the door, because I will have set myself up for a fall."

The fact is, the marketplace is constantly evolving, and it requires ongoing monitoring and study to keep ahead of the curve. This is the challenge and the fascination that keeps people like Ray Morgan plugging away.

Try it first, in a modest way, before deciding to commit to a career.

Market Research

Market research is something you will do a lot of, even though your job title may not reflect it. Product managers, marketing managers, and salespeople all conduct a great deal of market research, for the simple reason that they are continually meeting with customers and finding out what they want.

The process begins with the realization that you need to learn something about your existing and potential customers.

Once you have determined what you need to find out, you decide who *does* know and determine the best ways to contact them. These methods may include any or all of the following:

Focus groups

Direct mail

Telephone research

In person interviews (including scheduled appointments, door-to-door cold calling, and mall intercepts)

Once you have selected the vehicle, it is time to determine what constitutes a valid sample—something that varies enormously from one industry to another.

Research that you develop yourself or hire others to conduct is known as *primary* research. If, on the other hand, there is an existing body of knowledge that can tell you what you need to know, (such as U.S. census data) it is called *secondary* research.

Most of the time, secondary data costs less to acquire than primary, but you need to be certain that it is both relevant and current.

There are times when you and your fellow employees are simply too involved emotionally with the product, and you are unable to conduct your research objectively. Or, you just may not have the time to do it yourselves.

Either way, you need to avail yourself of the services provided by market researchers, either firms or contract labor.

Most marketing research positions are part time, and the pay is usually low. However, they are always hiring, you can gain a great deal of experience in a relatively short time, and the basic education requirements for entry-level positions are minimal.

The key to success in market research is to be neutral and not let your own bias creep into the proceedings. What matters are the opinions of the people you are querying, not yours.

The higher the education level of the people you are seeking information from, the better the research will be, because they will not be afraid that the interview will turn into a high-pressure sales call. They will understand how the process works and, if they have the time, they frequently enjoy being questioned. This is particularly true if they are going to be paid (a frequent occurrence with focus groups) and/or receive some other incentive (a gift certificate or a free meal, for example).

A part-time job with a market research firm (or with an ad agency that conducts research) will quickly teach you how the process works. You will deal with a variety of subjects and research instruments. For example, a typical four-hour shift may include the following:

1. A survey on cheese buying habits and preferences (You are interested in what consumers buy, and where they buy it.)

2. Questions concerning an upcoming ballot issue. (Be particularly careful about not showing how you feel.)

3. Probing the thoughts of a group of frequent flyers in terms of how they feel about a given airline's program. (Particularly in relation to other airlines' offerings.)

4. Calling businesses to find out how they choose janitorial services. (Note: Generally, business-to-business marketing research is easy to do, because the people you are talking to understand that the research is designed to improve things that help them in their work.)

Just working that shift will give you a look at different instruments and acquaint you with a number of very different groups of people. The key questions for you are:

1. Can you remain neutral and yet enthusiastic about the surveys?
2. Are you able to talk with very different types of people?
3. Can you make your quotas?
4. Is this what you want to do every day?

Several months of part-time work will give you the answers to these questions. If all four are "yes," it is time to begin language training and to study marketing formally (a course in research techniques and a survey course in marketing) and informally (reading textbooks and articles on the subject).

You will need to decide whether to seek full-time employment or contract employment with one or more firms, or you may even want to go into business for yourself. Before you decide, read Chapters 6 and 7 of this book.

It is easy to explore market research, simply by taking a part-time position with a marketing research company, an ad agency conducting research, or a polling company. Start with the classifieds, but don't overlook employment agencies.

Make it clear that you are seeking part-time work so that you can test the waters before committing to a career. Most places will be only too glad to give you a trial. The position won't pay much—usually an hourly rate plus mileage for travel—but you will be paid something while you are learning what you need to know.

You will also be able to test your selling skills, as there will be times when you have a quota to meet, time is running out, and the person you are talking to needs to be convinced that their opinion is important and that completing the interview is a worthwhile endeavor for them.

Sales and marketing careers are challenging, creative, and pressure-packed. If you can handle the pressure, however, any of the careers in sales and marketing we have looked at are very rewarding. Good people are always in demand and, thanks to a high turnover, entry-level positions are there for the taking.

Once you have established yourself in the domestic marketplace, you are ready to look at the international sector. In the next chapter, we will show you how to build your portfolio.

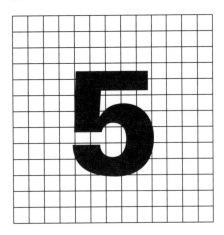

BUILDING YOUR PORTFOLIO

CHAPTER OBJECTIVES
Upon completion of this chapter, you should be able to:

1. Assess your life experience with an eye toward making you more marketable in the international sector

2. Take steps to eradicate any deficiencies in your experience

3. Prepare a portfolio that will enable you to begin seeking work in the field of your choice

"Be an expert" is sound advice. But how do you become an expert when no one is hiring?

Well, as the story of Maxine in the preceding chapter indicates, you can start at zero and really develop your qualifications over a period of time.

The fact is, though, most of us do not have to start at zero. We tend to have some marketable skills, but we probably do not value them as much as we should. This is particularly true of skills that come easily to us.

THE VALUE OF KNOWLEDGE AND EXPERIENCE

An artist I know has a hard time putting a price tag on his paintings because he does not have a "name" yet. He told me about a reasonably well-known artist whom he had met at a summer resort a few years ago. The artist was dashing off sketches of people and charging them $150. He told my friend, "I'm charging $25 for the sketch, and $125 for my name! Keep in mind that, in addition to the 15 to 20 minutes of direct work, there's another nearly 30 years of experience behind it."

What is the time that you have put in worth? One new consultant helped a client accomplish a few fairly major things rather rapidly. He said, "Really, all I did was make a few phone calls—so how much can I charge for *that*?" I pointed out to him that he not only had known whom to call, but that his calls were returned. I said, "The contents of your Rolodex is your stock in trade, and it took you years to build it up and establish yourself. Charge accordingly." Don't learn the value of your knowledge the hard way. Take this advice and do not go through a prolonged period of working for less than your fair market value!

What skills do *you* have? A former student of mine is a computer whiz. That alone makes him valuable to his employer, but better yet, he is a very patient person and is able to teach others.

He saw that there was not a good career path for him with his company and that he was likely to be stuck conducting tutorials for the firm for the rest of his career. He said, "I knew that I wanted to teach, but I wanted more free time, and I also wanted some variety." Together we mapped out a course of action.

First of all, he was well known within his company, but not outside it. He needed to establish himself as an expert in the eyes of a wider audience. The first step was to offer an introductory computer course for complete novices. He located a community school that had an education program and several PCs.

Starting small, he offered introductory PC training for a few people at a time. He made very little money, but he was on his way.

In time, he branched out at his first school and began teaching more specialized courses. The school promoted the classes, and he began to develop a "name." This led to another school's approaching him, and he soon was teaching at two places.

Inevitably, students would say, "I wish we had someone like you at our company." This led him to a major crossroad: Should he go out on his own and do contract work? This would provide him with some flexibility in terms of scheduling, as well as variety, because he would be moving around. On the other hand, getting started as an independent contractor is not exactly risk-free, so he has some serious thinking to do. The main point is, he started to build his portfolio without leaving his present job.

"Ad Exec to Set Up Shop in Moscow,"[1] was the headline for a newspaper article describing how a local advertising executive, Cheryl Shaul, who had founded a successful ad agency, was opening a branch in Moscow where she would provide " 'niche marketing' for U.S. and other western companies."

Ms. Shaul had started her agency nine years earlier, one year after she completed her studies in marketing and economics at the University of Wyoming. "It started with one client...an engineering firm, who'd hired her to coordinate marketing. 'There was another client and another, and that's how it grew,' she said." At the time of her move to Moscow, her firm's annual billings are "about $3.5 million."

"Within two years she expects the...branch to be self-sufficient enough that she'll turn it over to a Russian native who will act as an executive vice president. Then she'll head to new territories. 'With the technology that's available, I can go see the world,' she said. 'I'll be free to do business wherever I want to.'"

---

[1] Lynn Bronikowski, "Ad Exec to Set Up Shop in Moscow," *Rocky Mountain News,* November 13, 1994, 104A.

Hard work and talent are what enabled Ms. Shaul to succeed, and it is significant that she established herself in the domestic marketplace before going international.

It is also worth noting that she started with *one* client, which is, after all, all you need to begin.

YOUR CAREER INVENTORY

It is time for you to create a career inventory for yourself. Include everything, from your freshman year in high school forward, that can help you land a job.

Academic and Other Learning

Every course with career implications you have taken should be included in your inventory. This also includes non-scholastic training, such as seminars at work and training sessions conducted by various groups and individuals. These courses should be grouped by category, rather than dates, although you should note the dates you completed the courses. That way, if you are asked in an interview, "When did you take this course?" you will have the answer.

At first glance, a given course may not be construed as job-related. Let's look at the critical categories: (The categories marked with an asterisk have particular relevance where an international job search is concerned.)

Technical training
Communications (written and oral)
Foreign languages*
History*
Sociology*
Anthropology*
Geography*
Economics*
Geopolitics*
Business

If you have old textbooks and handouts, keep them. Also, save relevant books and materials from courses you are taking now and in the future.

Newspaper and magazine articles can be of significant value in keeping your knowledge current. Check the television listings for relevant shows and watch and tape them.

It is also worth your while to listen to National Public Radio's "Morning Edition" and/or "All Things Considered." The programs will give you the kind of in-depth news people in other countries take for granted.

If you have access to a shortwave receiver, listen to the English language broadcasts of foreign stations, and you will appreciate just how little news we actually get in the United States.

Your initial training in each area provided you with a method for pursuing knowledge on a lifelong basis. It is up to you to do this. Keep in mind that people from other countries appreciate the process of acquiring knowledge and respect individuals who are committed to learning, because they know that education does not stop when you earn a certificate or a degree. In fact, that is why graduations are referred to as "commencement exercises," because the graduates are making a new beginning.

Reviewing what you have already studied is both an encouraging and a humbling exercise. Like the rest of us, you are humbled by acknowledging how much there still is that you don't know. At the same time, you are greatly encouraged by that realization, because you have been provided by your education with the means for going after that knowledge. You will never learn everything, but the ongoing pursuit of knowledge is its own reward, as you will derive enormous satisfaction every time you realize that you have learned something new and significant.

In an ideal world, every time we come across a box where we are to write in our occupation, we should use the word "student," because we should all be striving to learn more and more. Unfortunately, many people conclude that their education stopped when they left school.

People who have stopped learning hold no interest for foreigners. People from other countries are amazed when they meet Americans who are not availing themselves of the readily-accessible training the United States offers.

Corporations that have made educational benefits available to their employees for many years have found, more often than not, that these benefits are not used because people don't "have the time" to go to school. Ironically, now that so many places are "down-sizing," people are using their benefits to try to make themselves more employable.

Many students are rushing to complete degrees and are cramming for college placement (CLEP) exams to help them complete their "studies" as quickly as possible. CLEPs do have their place. They are superb for people who have a sound body of knowledge in a given area and want to devote their time to studying at a higher level. Unfortunately, too many students who are able to cram for the test and pass it do not realize that the "knowledge" they acquired, without reinforcement, vanishes within a matter of weeks.

I have interviewed people who scored an "A" on a marketing exam who cannot even begin to discuss the subject. Yet, because the grade is on their transcript, they expect to be entrusted with marketing responsibilities!

Frankly, if you are not continuing to learn, your transcript, no matter how impressive, will not help. Your lack of intellectual curiosity will quickly be discerned in an interview with a foreign firm, and you will not get the job.

Our nation's intellectual laziness has cost us a great deal, but this does not have to happen to you. Happily, foreign firms are particularly willing to view applicants as individuals so, you will have an opportunity to demonstrate that you are not looking for shortcuts, academic or otherwise, and that you will be around, still learning and growing, for the long haul.

Work and Volunteer Experience

Generally, people don't have much difficulty listing the jobs they have held. It is important, however, to take each job apart and list all of your activities, including committees you may have served on, temporary assignments, and so on. All of these things can have relevance as you put your portfolio together.

Volunteer work and internships may be overlooked because they are unpaid. Don't fall into this trap. If you did something, whether you were paid or not, it has experiential value.

Volunteering can also acquaint you with the nuts and bolts of a field that you may want to enter. If you do decide the field is for you, you already have people with whom you have worked who will write reference letters for you. These letters can greatly enhance your chances for gaining acceptance into schools, training programs, and entry level positions.

If you worked on a project as a volunteer or a paid worker, make sure that you have examples of it for your portfolio. For example, you may have helped to translate a shelter's manual for residents into Spanish. If so, keep a copy to show, for example, to an interviewer from a foreign firm that requires a good working knowledge of written as well as spoken Spanish.

In short, just about everything you have studied or done from high school onward has potential when it comes to your portfolio.

When you complete a volunteer project or an internship, get a general, "To Whom It May Concern" letter from a person who is familiar with your work (or more than one, if possible). Thank the writer profusely, and stay in touch. Down the road, you may need the person to write a letter to a specific individual, and by keeping your name current with your reference writers you are networking, and this may open a door or two.

Teach classes, write articles for newspapers (even the small neighborhood weeklies), and volunteer to serve on committees. All of these activities afford you an opportunity to build your body of knowledge and make your name better known to people who may be in a position to help you.

On a regular basis, even if you are happy where you are, review your portfolio and match your experience with the criteria listed in attractive classified ads. This is a risk-free activity that will enable you to address your shortcomings before they can cost you a job.

These reviews will also allow you the opportunity to add to your portfolio things you may have forgotten the first time around. Finally, the reviews will reacquaint you with yourself and help you to acknowledge that you have indeed studied useful subjects and had valuable experiences.

All interviewers tend to regard favorably people who have a healthy amount of self-respect, and this is particularly true in the international sector. Often, we tend to denigrate our own efforts and intelligence, which is self-defeating.

The portfolio is useful as you prepare to write a cover letter and rearrange your resume. It is also a handy way to review your career prior to interviewing for a new position.

The people whose stories are told earlier in this chapter both started at "zero" many years ago. They did their work, both in and out of the classroom, and they built impressive portfolios. You have the opportunity to follow their example and produce a winning portfolio of your own. All it requires is a willingness to keep on learning and a lot of hard work.

"PERMANENT" OR CONTRACT EMPLOYMENT?

CHAPTER OBJECTIVES
Upon completion of this chapter, you should be able to:

1. Identify the key differences between "permanent" and contract employment

2. Determine which of the two you prefer

I see a lot of students who do not have much experience and expect to make a lot of money in the first year. Perhaps they should ask, 'How much will I make in five years?' instead of looking at the first salary.[1]

—Dr. Humberto Valencia

VIEWING THE JOB MARKET REALISTICALLY

A college of pharmacy used to run a classified ad that began with, "Pharmacists Don't Start at the Bottom!" I found it offensive. To me, it seems that being a pharmacist would be a rewarding profession, as it is part of the healing arts. Instead, the school seemed to feel that money would be the primary motivator for someone to enter the profession.

Certainly, the vast majority of people would like to make more money, but many of us would be unwilling to change professions in order to do so because we have gravitated toward careers that afford us intangible satisfactions, and we would be loathe to give up these satisfactions to do something we didn't like for more money.

Everything we have dealt with thus far in this book has been designed to make you a more desirable employee. However, as the old saw goes, "There's no substitute for experience."

Wherever you obtain your degrees, the fact is, when you first graduate you have not proven yourself to your new employer, and past successes, academic or otherwise, are no guarantee that you will succeed in a new setting.

A linguist I know was on a translating assignment in Eastern Europe, when he came across a graduate of one of our top law schools. This individual wanted to charge clients a huge amount of money to negotiate for them. There was only one problem—he didn't really speak the language!

Yes, he had "studied" it, but he had received what used to be called "Gentlemen's Cs," meaning that he was passed through without really being forced to learn anything. He applied English rules to Russian and made no

[1] Dr. Humberto Valencia, in a careers outlook portfolio from Thunderbird: The American Graduate School of International Management, 45–46.

attempt to change tenses, simply shoehorning words into an English-based sentence. The people with whom he came in contact were offended, and he was unable to do any business.

Yet, if you looked at his resume, he appeared to be qualified. After all, he had "studied" Russian at a first-rate university.

Even if his Russian had been superb, he had never negotiated with someone from Russia. His client would still pay while he learned to do so. Many fine students tend to overlook the fact that until you accumulate some on-the-job experience, you are of minimal worth to a client or employer.

Gwen Lawton, a senior personnel executive, never ceases to be amazed at the graduates of various business schools who, while still fanning the ink dry on their diplomas, inquire about senior positions and put their expected salary in the mid to upper range of the national average.

"They may have a B.S. in finance, from a very fine school," she said, "and they may have served a summer internship with a large bank, which is also very good. However, the position they feel they are qualified for is already filled by someone with a Ph.D. and 20 years' experience, who is making less money than the student's expecting!" Gwen added that when entry-level jobs are offered to promising applicants, they frequently reject them to search for "something better."

Face the facts: The world of work is largely a buyer's market. No one owes you a job, and, in most cases, many other resumes, many of them from highly experienced people, will be considered along with yours. Don't panic however. Employers *will* take a chance on a comparative neophyte who displays potential, provided that the applicant's approach is realistic.

DETERMINING YOUR NEEDS

I have purposely refrained from putting salary ranges into this book. That is because these ranges are averages, and are much too broad to even begin to deal with specific situations. What matters most is what you need to make in order to make a position worthwhile to you.

In order to determine what you need to make, you should put a budget together. Include everything:

Food:	Include eating out
Clothing:	Include dry cleaning and repairs
Transportation:	How old is your car? How much will it cost, including insurance increases, to replace it? What are your commuting costs for the proposed job? Also, even with a mileage reimbursement, your car will age rapidly if you have to use it in conjunction with your work.
Housing:	Will you rent or buy? Anticipate increases in insurance, real estate taxes, and monthly payments.

Entertainment:	What do you like to do? How often? What does it cost? Include vacations.
Education:	Consider education costs for yourself and significant others. How much do you need to lay aside for books, tuition, travel, living expenses, and fees?
Insurance:	Consider life, health, and dental insurance.
Savings:	What will it cost you to maintain your present (or desired) lifestyle when you retire? How much do you need to save on a regular basis to make this happen?
Other:	Consider such expenses as day care, support for aging parents, and charitable contributions.

You also need to budget your time. Will this position afford you sufficient free time to have a life of your own outside of work?

The next step is to ask yourself if you are willing to relocate. If so, where will you go, and where are you not willing to live and work? This is something that you need to discuss with those who are closest to you, because your choice affects them.

Do the organization's values square with your own? If they do, and the salary and working conditions meet your needs, you are well on your way to a successful arrangement. If they do not, you are likely to be unhappy eventually, no matter how much money you make.

CORPORATE VERSUS CONTRACT EMPLOYMENT

We appear to be heading toward a 50/50 split between contract and "regular" corporate employees. (Some estimates indicate that this will be true by the year 2000.)

Many people feel more secure if they have "permanent" employment. But, in an era of mergers, acquisitions, and technological advances, is any position really permanent?

Let's look at banking. For many years, it was a stable profession. The pay was not sensational in most cases, but layoffs were few, and the benefits were usually first-rate. Now, with the exception of a few highly specialized positions, banking is no longer a high-growth industry in terms of employment. This is particularly true of international banking.

In addition to mergers and acquisitions, the use of interactive computers has eliminated many jobs. For example, in the not-so-distant past, in order to transfer funds, check balances, and so on a customer had to call during business hours and talk to one or more people, depending upon the complexity of the institution.

These days, a customer "talks" to a computer, and can do it 24 hours a day, every day of the year. The people with whom customers used to speak have been laid off and, because they are gone, so is their former supervisor and, in all likelihood, the person in human resources who used to administer their benefits packages.

Computers very quickly amortize, and they keep right on working. Ultimately, they lower the cost of goods sold, which affords firms more latitude in pricing and/or investment decisions, including new product development.

Computers don't need holidays or raises and, properly programmed and maintained, they tend to eliminate variation, which is the curse of quality control. In short, they benefit everyone, with the exception of the people they replace (and their families and people who do business with them.) This may not be "fair," but it is reality, and needs to be acknowledged.

If you are offered "permanent" employment, and it meets your needs, by all means, accept it. I suggest, however, that you have a contingency plan in place before anything comes along to threaten your employment.

Even though you are employed, continue to read the classifieds regularly —but not at your desk! Check industry and function-specific publications, the dailies (particularly their weekend editions) and *The Wall Street Journal*. These will give you a good overview of the present job market.

It is also helpful to think like a consultant, and look at your own company as a potential client. What services could you perform for them on a contract basis if you lost your "permanent" job or decided to go into business for yourself?

Have a plan for what you will be doing five to ten years down the road if you remain with your present employer, and have a backup plan or two if you suddenly find yourself laid off.

Keep in mind that layoffs happen to good people, too. Often firms have to cut the payroll down to an affordable size. Being laid off is no reflection on you as a person. The critical thing is to be ready, and to put your contingency plan into action as soon as possible.

Contract work scares a lot of people. In fact, they tend to react to it the way most people do when a position as a commission-only sales rep is offered: "What if it doesn't work out?" they ask.

Well, a lot of "permanent" jobs don't work out either. Don't worry about contract work. Yes, it is scary, at first, but it has many distinct advantages to it, and the pluses far outweigh the minuses.

1. Contract work is for a specified period.
   Con: That means that you are only guaranteed employment for a limited time.
   Pro: Yes, and if you are good, the company will offer to renew the contract. And if you are really good, you will be free to sign a new, more lucrative contract elsewhere.
2. Contract work is limited in scope.
   Con: I used to do a lot of things on the job. The contract only calls for me to do a few specific things.
   Pro: These are the things you tend to do best. Now you are free to pursue these activities full time, instead of having to drop them for, as the job descriptions say, "other duties as assigned."

3. Contract workers are not regular employees.

    Con: I am used to being part of the team, not an outsider. I don't count!

    Pro: When you were part of the team, were you low on the organization chart? Now you are a professional expert.

The satisfaction of having one's work receive high priority cannot be overstated. Instead of being one of many among the "permanent" staff members, you are a pro, and your time is worth money. Thus, you are able to do real work as a contract consultant, and it is infinitely preferable to down time due to game-playing by those above you on the organization chart.

If you are good, the contracts keep coming, and you can make income predictions with a high degree of certainty. After all, the contract clearly spells out what you will be making during its existence.

You can also build in additional revenue to pay for your benefits package. This is a very important consideration. A regular corporate benefits package including health insurance, retirement plans, and so on can be worth at least a fourth of what a person's base compensation is. So, if you are in business for yourself, it is important that you build this into the cost for your services.

Be realistic. The market may not bear the cost of a benefits package similar to corporate benefits. However, your rate of compensation should cover at least a basic insurance plan.

Generally, the "going rate" for the type of services you offer already has the benefits' costs built into it. Keep this in mind when you are quoting your own rate.

A contract employer is usually prepared for this, and does not begrudge you the cost of a benefits package. After all, "permanent" employees expect raises, promotions, and pensions as well as health, dental, vision, and life insurance. As a contract worker, you are only getting your basic rate, for the duration of the contract. When the contract period is over, the firm owes you nothing. The fact that part of your compensation goes into "benefits" paid for by you does not concern them.

RESUMES, COVER LETTERS, AND INTERVIEWS

Whether you are seeking contract or "permanent" employment, your approach is largely the same. First read the classifieds. There are two types of ads, those that identify the firm, and those that do not. The latter are known as "blind" ads.

Blind ads make sense from the firm's standpoint. First, they eliminate time-consuming phone calls from prospective applicants. Second, if they choose not to reply to your letter and resume, you don't know for certain who rejected you, so you don't have any negative feelings toward the firm.

A blind ad asks you to respond by mailing to a box or contacting an employment agency. The agency has been engaged to go through the costly process of screening applicants and coming up with the best people to interview. In fact, your very first interview is likely to be with a representative of the agency, rather than the firm with the vacancy.

Over time, you will learn to recognize "voices" in classified ads. Firms tend to write all of their want ads in the same style. It is amusing to find an ad that identifies the firm in the same issue of a publication as a blind ad written in the exact same style. When this happens, play along, and do what the ad asks you to do.

The Resume

Read the classified ad several times. What, exactly, is the company looking for? How does this fit with what is on your current resume and with your career goals? Will this job, if it is all that it seems to be, take you in what you perceive to be the right direction? If it is, it is time to review your resume.

How does your resume present you? What items need to be reworded to better match what the prospective employer is looking for? Keep in mind that we are talking about varying presentation, not altering the facts. For example, you may want to begin or end a given section by emphasizing things that are relevant to the firm's needs.

Remember that promising resumes tend to be saved, so if you have applied to a given firm before, your old resume is likely to be on file, and it may end up with your new one. It's all well and good if they pretty well match up with each other, as prospective employers appreciate the need for making the most of what you've done and know in terms of stressing different things when applying for different jobs, but if the two are wildly different, you will never get called for an interview.

The Cover Letter

The cover letter is used to tie the ad and your resume together. It stresses why you are a good applicant for this particular position. It points out things that might not be apparent at first glance from your resume.

For example, your volunteer experience may be pertinent to the job qualifications. Unless you take the time to tell about this experience, however, your resume is likely to end up in the rejects pile.

The cover letter shows that you and the job are a superb match. A lot of thought needs to go into the letter, because this is your chance to arouse the company's interest in you.

Once again, the goal is to secure an interview, and, at this point, all you need to do is convince the screener that you are someone worth talking to.

The career inventory discussed in the previous chapter comes into play here, as you review everything you have done as a paid worker or a volunteer, as well as every course and seminar you have taken. This will provide you with maximum firepower as you write the cover letter.

In the letter, tell why the position appeals to you, and cite specific examples of experience and education that you believe make you a viable candidate. Be very positive, and say you are looking forward to meeting with the recipient to learn more about the position.

An upbeat letter that uses specifics is much more likely to be successful than a cookie-cutter epistle from a resume writing service. Letters and resumes prepared by these services all look and sound alike, because they use standard form templates and plug in the names and other information.

It makes sense that *you* are the best writer for the task of writing your cover letter, as you are the one who is going to have to land the position during the one or more interviews that ensue when a letter and resume have elicited a favorable response. When the interviewer is able to match your voice in person with the tone and substance that attracted him or her in the initial written contact, you are off to a very good start.

The Interview

The interview requires significant preparation. Most interviewers appreciate conservative attire and an absence of fragrances. Seeking work is, after all, serious business. A conservative approach is appreciated even more in the international sector.

Do your homework! Review your career and think through your answers to the questions you know the interviewer will ask. A good way to do this is through silent study—simply sitting down and going over the questions and your answers in your mind. A rule of thumb is that if your answers do not make sense to you, they probably will not make a favorable impression on the interviewer. By taking the time to prepare, you have an opportunity to maximize your chances of success.

Learn as much as you can about the company and its products. Also devote time to learning about the firm's home country, even if the position you are applying for is in the United States.

Review what you know about your own country. After all, because most international positions are likely to at least start here, it is vital that you be an expert on how business is done in the United States.

A fairly common technique, even with domestic firms, is to slide a manager into the receptionist's chair prior to an interviewee's arrival. This enables the firm to assess firsthand how you treat underlings. Keep this in mind: there is never a time when you are not being assessed. Even when it really is the receptionist behind the desk in the waiting area, he or she is frequently called in afterward to comment upon an interviewee's deportment.

The interview will have its own rhythm, and the interviewer will determine what that rhythm is. He or she will afford you numerous opportunities to display your skills and it is important that you listen for the clues the interviewer gives you.

The interviewer will tell you things that may contradict your preconceived ideas. Listen carefully, and adapt to the changes as they arise.

Remember, we think at about five to six times the rate of normal speech, so there is time to listen and adjust your responses.

Good interviewers are trained to ask open-ended questions—questions that cannot be answered with a simple yes or no. So, instead of asking, "Do you like your present job?" an interviewer may say, "What aspects of your current job do you like?"

In asking the question, the interviewer is leading you to come up with at least two things you like about the job, and will expect you to elaborate on your response.

International screeners will likely probe more deeply into your world view, philosophy, and diplomatic skills than will a domestic job interviewer. This is because most foreigners tend to have a broader view of the world, a deeper appreciation for what they think about life (and, generally, a better ability to express this verbally), and a greater ability to adapt to different cultures than do their American counterparts.

In a presentation to my global marketing class, Steve Mulvihill, who among other things served as president of the U.S. affiliate of a German-owned company, said, "You have to be something of a chameleon in international business. This is because you will move from one culture to another, and you need to be able to adapt rapidly to new circumstances."

Steve also stressed the need for simple, direct (but not blunt) language when it comes to discussing terms, to reduce the chance of a misunderstanding. "Humor and slang are always dangerous," Steve said, "because there's a good chance that you'll be taken seriously when you're joking, and the slang won't be understood either."

He continued, "Even when the other person speaks English, it isn't the same English, and there are bound to be lots of mistakes." He also cautioned against talking too much, as most other cultures employ periods of silence to reflect upon what has been said, prior to speaking further.

More than one interview may be required to land the job. Be prepared for this, and understand that you are operating in a buyer's market, so the employer determines the rules.

Ultimately, if the position's offered, it is up to you to determine if it honestly meets your needs. If it does not, don't take it!

The distinction between contract and "permanent" employment really does not mean a lot any more. In the not so distant past, "permanent" employment included a benefits package and, theoretically, at least, an opportunity to advance. Today, many organizations have cut back on benefits and have also reduced long-range opportunities, because so many really good people are available to work on a contract basis.

As long as your compensation under the contract enables you to pay for your own benefits package, I think that the pluses of contract employment outweigh those of having a "regular, permanent job." If you are good, more contracts will be forthcoming, with more flexibility and better compensation, and that is not a half bad way of going through your working life.

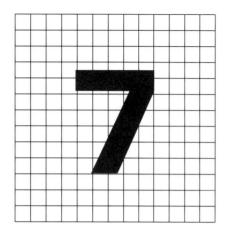

ENTREPRENEURS IN INTERNATIONAL BUSINESS

CHAPTER OBJECTIVES
Upon completion of this chapter, you should be able to:

1. Assess your potential for entrepreneurship or intrapreneurship

2. Draft a business plan

3. Take the first steps toward reaching your goal

Radio and television business reporter Keith Weinman once began a series on entrepreneurship with the provocative question, "Do you have what it takes to mind your own business?" That is a fair question, and one that you will be better able to answer when you have read this chapter.

WHAT IT TAKES TO START A BUSINESS

Entrepreneurs take risks, because most new businesses fail. Starting a new business is not for everyone, because there are no guarantees that a going concern will be the end result, no matter how hard the persons involved work. If the marketplace fails to show sufficient interest, the business dies.

The stress scares off most people, but thankfully, there are still some hardy souls who are willing to put themselves on the line and bring new products and services to market. If it were not for people like them, little or no progress would be made.

Before we go any further, the issue of *intra*preneurship must be addressed. Intrapreneurs are people who are able to convince their present employers to fund new ventures. They have to face the same obstacles as entrepreneurs, particularly when it comes to securing funding. Intrapreneurs, like entrepreneurs, may have to surrender a fairly high percentage of the profits in return for the money required to start the venture, but they are in a somewhat stronger position when it comes to hiring people. (We will have more on that later in the chapter.)

Venture capitalists, bankers, and corporations who are willing to put up money have one basic question, "What guarantees can you provide that you will pay us back on time, at an acceptable rate of return?" This is a fair question, as it is, after all, their money. They will grill you, and thoroughly examine your business plan. Even if they are very interested, they may demand additional information, including a more fleshed-out plan. This will require time, money, and effort on your part (not to mention emotional "capital"). If you are not up to the job of fund raising, you will have to use your own money.

People who can run their own businesses have a great deal of determination and staying power. They are not deterred by setbacks, and they have prepared themselves financially to make the attempt to start and grow a business.

Can you deal with the stress of running your own business? Keep in mind that you are going to have to do more work than you have ever done before, particularly during the start-up phase. Evenings, weekends, and even holidays may find you working away, often performing tasks that could be done more productively by others, if only you had a sufficient cash flow to be able to hire them.

You may work for years, and never make a cent. In addition to working for little or no pay, you may lose your own money directly, by pouring it into the business, and indirectly, by not being available for paying positions with other organizations. To be blunt: The odds are against you.

If the foregoing discourages you to the point of deciding against entrepreneurship, you have avoided the hardships involved. If it does not, you have the makings of an entrepreneur, and it is time to get to work.

PREPARING A BUSINESS PLAN

A business plan is a must and, in addition to being a basic requirement for getting capital, it is a helpful exercise for you, because it forces you to evaluate your ideas objectively and to determine in advance just how much time and effort are required.

Here's a fairly standard model for a business plan's table of contents:

Executive Summary
Company Background
Company Products
Customer Base
Industry Background
Marketing Strategies
Management
Financial History
Financial Projections

Herbert C. Cohen, president of Monaco Associates, Inc., says, "Rest assured that everyone will read the table of contents and the executive summary, just to be sure that everything's there. After that, they tend to read only the parts that are within their areas of expertise."

Herb's points are well taken. First of all, the decision to lend or not to lend is usually made by a committee, and, second, not everyone is going to read your entire plan.

Let's walk through the plan, which may be labeled "Confidential Investment Summary," item by item:

Executive Summary: The executive summary is an abridged version of your entire plan. It encapsulates the main features of the rest of your plan. Your readers want an overview here, one that hits the highlights and gives them a good general picture of what you intend to do. It needs to grab the reader, and it should not run more than two or three pages at most. So, hit the highlights of your plan.

Company Background: If yours is an existing company, and you are seeking the money to go international, provide a history of your firm. If not, what led to bringing this proposed venture into being?

Company Products: Again, if you have some history, go over it here. What have you done in the past? What kind of returns have you paid investors who funded your other products? If this is totally new, why have you decided to provide this particular product? (Note: Your product may be a service.)

Customer Base: Who will buy your product? How many of them are there? Where are they located? In the case of exporting, where do you intend to sell the product overseas? How will it be distributed? By whom? What are the laws and regulations you will need to comply with? What are the customers' current purchasing options? In other words, what else is on the market, and what will provide you with a competitive edge? Also, what is going on with your customers' local economy? Do they have the ability to purchase your product? To them, is it a luxury or a necessity?

Industry Background: Who are your competitors? This was touched upon briefly in the previous section, but now, go into detail. Will you be a innovator, a "me too" provider (offering something at a significant discount), or have you created something that no one else has, designed to penetrate and capture a small segment of the market that will not be lucrative enough to attract competition, but will allow you to make an acceptable profit?

Marketing Strategies: How will you make your potential customers aware of what your product is, what it will do for them, how much it costs, and where they can get it?

Management: The section on management provides resumes in narrative form, similar to what you would find in a baseball yearbook or a theater program. Hit the high points—Who are your key players? What skills do they bring to the venture? What is their educational background? What awards have they won? What are their greatest achievements? What, specifically, will they be doing to implement this plan? (Note: Standard resumes should also appear in your appendices, along with other material to support your claims.)

Financial History: How well have you and your management people handled money in the past, either with your present firm, or elsewhere? Indicate the rates of return you have earned for people (including employers) who have put up money for plans you have created and implemented.

Financial Projections: Usually, financial projections need to be carried out for a three to five-year period. Find out in advance what the people you are trying to raise money from want to see.

Generally, people who write business plans tend to be unduly optimistic and to ask for less money than they actually need. This may lead to the plan's being rejected out of hand because a knowledgeable potential investor says, "This isn't realistic." Or, you may get what you requested and be caught in the embarrassing position of having to raise more money in midstream. In this case you will probably have to pay a lot more for the additional money than you can ultimately afford (because the new investor knows you are desperate), if anyone will loan you money at all. Most new businesses fail, and they go under because they lack sufficient capital to make it through the start-up phase.

One business writer says, "You should usually spell out the risks in a proposal rather than minimizing them. There are even times when it's to your political advantage to *exaggerate* the risks."[1] This advice applies to business plans. Make it clear to your readers that you are aware of everything that can go wrong, and that you have planned for it. Put the risks in black and white, and ask for the money you need to guard against the risks. Too often, only rosy scenarios appear in business plans, and experienced investors are turned off by them.

Leading with the risks, and mentioning even the minor ones, is a good exercise for you, too, as it enables you to answer the question, "Do I really want to go through with this?" If your answer is yes, and you have enumerated the risks in your proposal, you will strike potential investors as someone who thinks things through and has the confidence (and the plan) to overcome adversity.

An instructor at a business seminar I attended said, "A plan should be readily understandable and concise." Actually, *any* business writing should be understandable and concise. A good approach is to remember a strategy discussed earlier, and to pretend that what you are writing is a telegram that is going to cost you $50 a word. Doing this, brevity is rather easy to achieve.

Management consultant Berle Larned suggests writing out your plan as quickly as possible, and then laying it aside for a few days. That will provide you with the nucleus for your first draft. Once you have written that, take it to someone who has no stake in the plan's outcome and whose opinion you trust (you may also want to have the reader sign a confidentiality agreement). If this person is able to understand your plan, you have a document that is likely to be read by potential investors.

---

[1] Jack Tarrant, *Business Writing with Style* (New York: John Wiley & Sons, 1991), 94.

CONSIDERATIONS FOR EXPORTERS

Frank Seffinger and Ron Lubbers are CPAs and small-business consultants. In one of their columns, they discussed key considerations for individuals and small firms who are interested in exporting:

> Before you can begin to export, and even before you do your market research,...give serious consideration to the commitment that exporting commands.
>
> The U.S. and Foreign Commercial Service suggests that you meet seven criteria before taking further steps in the process.
>
> - A corporate plan that outlines strong commitment at all levels of your management.
> - A strong position in your regional market.
> - A reference list of your major customers.
> - Good credit references and a good credit rating or a solid financial statement.
> - Adequate cash flow that can carry a foreign buyer or the ability to persuade a local banker to finance the sale on the seller's collateral credit.
> - At least two years of business experience and knowledge of your domestic and foreign competition.
>
> Also bear in mind that it takes at least a couple of years of diligent effort before you can begin to see success in your exporting efforts.
>
> As with any venture, it's important to understand the "do's and don'ts" of the process before you step into your new obligations....
>
> ITO [the International Trade Office] recommends that you:
>
> - Plan a solid marketing strategy. Here is where your market research is especially helpful.
> - Understand the legal aspects of trade in your target market.
> - Research your options carefully before making a commitment with an agent, distributor or other partner to sell your products.
> - Be aware of language misunderstandings, which are bound to arise. Avoid using jargon and slang.
>
> Some exporting mistakes are common no matter what the business industry or size. Avoid:
>
> - Attempting to enter too many markets at once. Target one or two to start, then expand only when they succeed.
> - Insisting on doing it "your way." Cultural traditions of the country you are dealing with could cause serious friction in your export relationships.
> - Neglecting your domestic customers.[2]

---

[2] Frank Seffinger and Ron Lubbers, "Meet Seven Key Requirements to Export Successfully," *Rocky Mountain News*, July 27, 1994, business sec.

Company Size

One frequently asked question concerning doing business overseas is, don't you have to be a big company to do business internationally? The answer is no. All business sizes fit in this marketplace. For example, I met one of the members of (literally) a mom and pop doll manufacturing firm a number of years ago. They produced a line of eminently collectible porcelain dolls. Together with a small number of employees, they were able to service a fairly large group of international customers. They had discovered that there is a mark of distinction to something from the United States (remember, overseas *we* are the exotic foreigners), and they had no difficulty tapping into various markets.

In most foreign countries, visiting the United States is high on the wish list of most people when they are asked about their dreams of foreign travel. So, wearables and collectibles that can be readily identified as being of U.S. origin are in demand.

You have only to travel abroad to see how many U.S. schools and products are "advertised" on various items of apparel to understand just how great the demand is.

How To Begin

In beginning an exporting business, first of all, see if your city or state has an international trade office. Then, get in touch with the U.S. Department of Commerce. You will find them in the government pages of your phone book.

Trade offices and the Department of Commerce have one goal: to help the United States create and maintain a favorable balance of trade. As you doubtless know, a country's balance of trade is considered favorable when the value of its exports exceeds the value of its imports. In recent years, the United States has had an unfavorable balance, so government entities, which have always been most helpful, are now even more eager to assist anyone who is willing to try exporting products or services. (By the way, trade offices and the U.S. Department of Commerce are also superb contacts if you want to import.)

In addition, embassies and consulates of the country with which you want to do business can be very helpful. Trade officers are charged with the responsibility of helping people in the host country who want to trade with their country. To find them, check the Yellow Pages under "Consulates and Foreign Government Representatives."

Collecting Payment

Actually, collections are frequently smoother and more certain in the international sector than they are domestically. While a domestic firm may not pay you after you have shipped the product, saying, "We've just filed bankruptcy under Chapter 11, how about settling for cents on the dollar?" foreign collections are often handled using letters of credit. *The Global Marketing Imperative* by Czinkota, Ronkainen, and Tarrant (Lincolnwood, IL: NTC, 1994), does a superb job of describing these instruments and their applications. The rest of the book is also a must read for anyone who is interested in doing business abroad.

THE IMPORTANCE OF TRAVELING

It is amazing how many people who say they want to do business internationally have not traveled. There is nothing like an on-site inspection to tell you what day-to-day life is like there. There are things that you can learn while posing as a tourist that will serve you in good stead.

For example, you will doubtless find Mexico City's heavy traffic described in any number of publications. However, not until you are actually on the scene can you truly appreciate just how much congestion there is.

A glance at population and income figures makes Mexico City look very attractive as a place to do business. Maps show many broad thoroughfares, so it would seem relatively easy for a sales rep in a car to get around and call on customers.

If you visited, however, you would readily realize just how many hours are wasted simply sitting in traffic, and you would quickly project your sales rep's number of in-person calls per day sharply downward.

Mexico City is one the best places on this planet to conduct all kinds of business, but, due to congestion, the pace is, of necessity, slow.

Certain Third World cities are notorious for their frequent power outages. Once again, in the abstract, this may not mean much to you. Once you have been in such a place, however, and you realize that virtually everything stops, frequently for hours at a time and often on a daily basis, you may have to readjust your figures for what "cheap" labor actually costs in such a setting.

There is also nothing like going through customs and immigration at various borders to understand just how bureaucratic some countries can be, and how difficult it is for foreigners to thread the maze. When you see this first hand, you will realize that you are going to need local assistance not only to set up your business, but to keep it going once you have secured legal approval to operate there.

Face the fact that if you are not thoroughly conversant with a given country, you are negotiating from a weak position. So, it is imperative that you travel there before beginning an international venture.

Do not go on a package tour, either. Instead, book yourself to and from the capital's airport, and make your own hotel reservations and ground transportation arrangements. Eat away from the tourist haunts, and do a great deal of walking, taking an up-close look at things. Do this more than once!

Study the language before going and, to the greatest extent possible, use it while you are there.

After two or three visits, combined with reading everything you can get your hands on concerning the country and doing business there, and continuing to study the language, you will have a good idea if it really is a place where you want to do business, and you will be in a better position to:

1. Secure funding because of your expertise
2. Locate and hire the right kind of representation in the target country
3. Continue to build upon what you have already learned

Walking around in the country will give you an idea of what kinds of establishments offer the kinds of things you would like to sell. You will also come away with a pretty good picture concerning who shops in these places, and what the competition is like.

If you do not take the time to go there in person, you are flying blind, and you are in danger of being victimized by people who are only too ready to take advantage of your ignorance..

Ironically, many such people are well-intentioned. They love their countries and want to promote trade, so they are likely to tell you the things they feel that you will want to hear, and gloss over the rest. After all, if a foreigner is willing to invest, why not "help" him or her?

This is particularly true where market research is concerned. Once again, you can avoid the pitfalls by doing some on-site work yourself, because you know specifically what it is that you need to learn about a potential market. Keep in mind that market research as we know it is not well refined in many countries, and you are the one who suffers if it is not conducted properly.

"Learn the language" is sound advice, and that also means making sure, even when English is being spoken, that you agree on meanings.

For example, my old company was once offered an "exclusive" marketing agreement with the largest vendor in a certain country. Everyone was excited until someone mentioned that this firm already represented our chief competitor. When queried more closely the vendor said, "By 'exclusive' I mean that your company does business only through my company in my homeland." When given our firm's definition of the word, namely that we would be the only company in our industry whom he would represent in his homeland, he laughed and said, "That will never work!" He added, "I've never heard of anything like what you've proposed!"

In many cases, intermediaries are necessary, not only to help you with the legal hurdles, but also with interpreting. In fact, if you are planning to go into business for yourself, be prepared to spend money up front. You will need the services of an attorney at some point, and, most likely, a CPA. It is also helpful to avail yourself of the abilities of a person who has international business experience. A good place to look is the Service Corps of Retired Executives (SCORE).

You can contact SCORE through the Small Business Administration. They will match you with someone who has experience in your general area, a person who can tell you from firsthand experience what can go wrong and how to avoid problems.

YOUR OFFICE

Many entrepreneurs, particularly those with corporate backgrounds who are accustomed to going to the office every day, open an office right away, using precious working capital. They negotiate a lease, put in the phones, buy the furniture and paintings, and subscribe to all the right magazines. Then, they sit and wait for the phone to ring.

Within a year, many of them are out of business, and the furniture, now "used" (although hardly anyone has seen it, let alone used it) brings next to nothing on the resale market.

Frankly, you do not need an office until you actually have a business. And, even then, you may still be able to have your office in your own home.

Home is the best place to start, because it requires the least amount of up-front expenditures. Ask yourself, honestly, what do you really need?

- A dedicated phone line? Perhaps, but maybe not at first.

- An answering machine, an answering service, or voice mail? The critical issue here is how detailed your messages are likely to be and how often you are likely to be away.

- A fax machine? To what extent will you be sending or receiving faxes? Good alternatives may be using a "community" fax in an office complex, or the faxing services of a nearby copying center.

- A post office box? Some people I know who live and work out of their rural homes maintain a city mailing address, which may be more reassuring to foreign clients, who want representation in major cities.

  Many places that rent post office boxes will allow you to use their street address and, instead of a box number, employ the term "suite" in your address. This is perfectly fine if you are not planning to meet customers in person at your mailing address.

- A copying machine? Here again, depending upon your volume, you may want to use a commercial outlet, many of which are now open 24 hours a day. Often, they also have fax machines and printing and full-color copying services, so you can use them as a full-service office, around the clock, which is particularly convenient when you are dealing with overseas clients.

- A personal computer or word processor? You will need a computer to keep financial and customer records as well as to produce correspondence and reports.

- A typewriter? Perhaps. They are very inexpensive, particularly used ones, and they are convenient when you have to complete forms with lots of boxes and copies.

- A shipping service? You will need a shipping service, and they abound. Many will come to your home. A better bet, though, may be using one that is a clearing house for several services. This firm may also offer P.O. boxes, copying, and other services, including being a U.S. Post Office substation. In addiiton to providing you with the best carrier for a particular parcel or communication, such places have the added benefit of getting you out of the house, which can help you to clear your head. Remember, one of the biggest things people miss when they have left a traditional office setting is daily interaction with coworkers. The people who run shipping and copying centers help to fill this important void.

- Business cards? Yes. Business cards are used commonly in the United States, but are particularly important in the international sector. Generally, be conservative, and pay the little bit extra for good quality. After all, the card represents *you*. The Japanese, for example, give and receive business cards with both hands, and read them very solemnly. In the international sector, it is common to have two-sided cards, with the English language information on one side, and the foreign language (including local contacts in that country) on the other. You will likely need the services of a good translator to do this, but it is worth the cost.

- Stationery? Yes. Keep in mind the possibilities for using foreign languages here (see the above section on business cards).

- Office supplies? Yes. Shop around. This is a highly competitive market.

- Office furniture? Most likely. Again, it pays to shop around, particularly at used office furniture stores. You can find some terrific bargains, because so many people wasted money on good furniture they really did not need and could not afford, and you can profit from their mistakes. Goodwill shops also have the occasional "steal," and it is worth your while to check.

Visit your local IRS office and pick up copies of all relevant publications pertaining to self-employment, including using a home office.

If you do not have an attorney, call your local bar association and ask about legal referrals. Lawyer referral services are available in some cities. These services will match you with the right type of legal specialist, and charge a minimal fee for the first session.

Friends and associates may also have good recommendations. Ultimately, the final decision is yours, and your comfort level is what really matters. Your attorney will advise you on the pluses and minuses of incorporation, partnerships, and so on.

Consulting a CPA is also a good idea. Check with friends and associates first, and also go through the Yellow Pages. Once again, choose a professional with whom you feel comfortable.

If you need a separate office from the start, or find, after working out of your home for a while, that you need a separate office, consider renting space in a suite of offices that specializes in leasing to a variety of clients.

Look in the Yellow Pages under "Office and Desk Space Rental Services." Most cities of any consequence have such establishments. They frequently provide secretarial and receptionist services, as well as communal faxes, copiers, and conference rooms, as well as dedicated phone lines.

Location may or may not be critical to your business. Happily, office rental establishments tend to be located in commercial districts and in or near major office parks, so you should be able to find space where you need to be.

The foregoing is all designed to save you time and money. New business ventures tend to fail because they are undercapitalized. Your initial working capital, wherever it comes from, should be expended frugally.

Obviously, it is possible for you to cost out everything we have discussed before making any commitments. Rental fees, hourly professional rates, and so on can all be quoted to you before you put together a preliminary budget. This exercise should be a sobering experience, because it spells out to you the overhead involved in going into business for yourself.

THE BENEFITS OF INTRAPRENEURSHIP

Intrapreneurship is a good way to avoid these start-up costs, because they will be borne by your present employer. As we saw earlier, you will still have to meet the same requirements to secure financing as you would in an entrepreneurial venture, but there are many pluses to going in-house, if your present employer is willing to fund such a venture.

If this is the case, you are dealing from real strength when it comes to hiring good people from within the organization. After all, although these people will have to leave their present jobs to join your venture, just as they would if you had become an entrepreneur, they can do so without leaving the company. This means that they will continue with their seniority and their benefits, and these are great bargaining chips for you.

Entrepreneurs have a more difficult time attracting good people because their new firm has no products and no history. It also does not have any cash flow, so salaries are a drain with no guarantees of return, so future salaries may simply not be there.

New ventures come and go like the tides, and their arrivals and departures frequently are unnoticed. On the other hand, a new venture launched by an existing firm of some consequence, particularly one with international possibilities, is news, so it is much easier to get coverage in the business press.

Although you surrender a great deal of the profits if you take the intrapreneurial route, the increased chances for success and the serenity that comes from having a larger entity backing you are usually worth it.

First, there are no guarantees that there will be any profits. Second, entrepreneurs frequently give up a lot of their initial profits (if any) to pay back the individuals and organizations that backed their venture in the first place. So, the payback to investors is pretty much the same either way, and I believe that you are better off choosing the intrapreneurial route if at all possible.

CAREERS IN CONSULTING

If you have established yourself as an expert in the domestic market, you are a prime candidate for working for an international firm, most likely right here in the United States.

Consultants understand local conditions and are in an excellent position to provide a wide variety of services, including sales, public relations, marketing research, and investing. Here's how one major U.S. conglomerate, Anheuser-Busch, approaches the international market:

> The company's efforts to expand its beer operations around the globe are enhanced by a detailed knowledge of a country's governmental and political environment. For these reasons, Anheuser-Busch has built a network of consultants in nations around the world to provide information and direction in helping the company deal with important local issues.[3]

Jesse Arman is a chartered financial consultant in the United States. He helps a variety of domestic clients to prepare investment portfolios designed to provide long-term income, particularly after they retire.

He sees an opportunity in the international sector for his services, and also believes that other professionals can expand their practices by serving foreign clients. Here are his comments:

> There is a statistically-supported historical tendency for foreign individuals and firms to seek refuge in U.S.-based investments (and dollars) during periods of turmoil overseas. They may be justifiably reluctant to invest in a thinly-traded stock on an overseas stock exchange, but no such reluctance exists regarding stocks traded on the "Big Board" (a euphemism for the 2,000 or so stocks listed on the New York Stock Exchange)....

> However, just as U.S. citizens are prohibited from directly owning most overseas stocks, foreign investors are precluded from direct ownership of certain U.S.-based investments.... There is a niche for U.S.-based investment advisors and accountants who can offer foreign clients information regarding overcoming these restrictions. Even with the almost immediate worldwide availability of financial information, it is still the case that U.S.-based investment professionals perform the highest quality fundamental analyses of U.S. corporations. Simply put, an investment analysis prepared by a local national is likely to be more complete than one prepared by a counterpart in another country....

> A foreign client would be best served by a *team* of advisors. The members of this group, realizing the inherent complexity of the situation, would each contribute specific expertise to the plan. Optimally, this team would consist of the financial planner, an accountant who is conversant with domestic taxation of foreign investors, and an attorney.

The beauty of having such a team is that every member can network with his or her own clients, spreading the word that the team is seeking international clients.

---

[3] "Anheuser-Busch Companies, 1994/1995," 32 (volume included in media kit).

A great many "international" attorneys do not travel much at all; except, perhaps, on vacations. As we learned when we looked at the investments analysis team, local lawyers are valued for their knowledge of the laws of their own nations, states, or provinces. They provide valuable legal assistance to foreign clients by staying where they are members of the Bar.

Attorneys network a great deal, and frequently have contacts nationally and internationally. Word of mouth, combined with news stories, is their best form of advertising. For example, several years ago, I wanted to effect the collection of a past-due account in the United Kingdom. A phone call to a local attorney with international connections led to a referral to a firm of solicitors in London. They, in turn, would refer their clients with problems in the United States to the attorney whom I had contacted originally.

So, networking is critical, no matter what your business is. Happily, we are predisposed to doing this anyway, and technology has greatly enhanced our ability to contact people all over the world. If you are in touch with people who live overseas, be sure to let them know what you do for a living and that you are eager to take on new clients.

Keep in mind that, whether they back you financially or not, your present employer might well be your first customer when you go into business for yourself. They know you, and you know what they need.

For example, a former student of mine was part of an in-house technical support team. His firm was planning to lay the team off, and contract for the support elsewhere. The team members got together and drafted a proposal. In return for reduced rates, the company agreed to fund the start-up costs for an entrepreneurial venture. The team continued to service their former employer's needs, and, once the initial seed money had been repaid, they owned their business outright and began charging their old firm a higher rate. Meanwhile, they had been making cold calls and had created a very nice client base. In short, this was a win-win proposition, as their old company cut costs even as it was helping the team to go into business for themselves.

YOUR INTERNATIONAL VENTURE

Look around you. What needs doing? In the case we just looked at, the team started with a domestic client and began prospecting elsewhere. In time, the word got out that they were both affordable and good. They were also open to the idea of taking their expertise on the road. This attitude led to their being asked to make proposals to service foreign clients, first through the clients' U.S.-based affiliates and, subsequently, overseas.

Home is the place to begin! You know the territory, literally and figuratively. If you are good at what you do, you price your goods or services fairly, and you network aggressively on an ongoing basis, the word will get around, and your business will grow and prosper.

As we discussed earlier in this book, many foreigners take a long-term view of things, so consultants and businesses that have some history are considered highly desirable.

The key to success in a business of your own is to be properly funded right from the start, and to be patient while you are working hard to establish yourself. Once you have established a good reputation, you will be in a position to receive serious consideration in the international marketplace.

If what you are offering is local expertise, it is important that you have a good list of references from people for whom you have been doing quality work for some time. That is what attracts potential overseas clients.

If your business deals with a product, it is imperative that you be well-established in the domestic market, having proved your ability to deliver a quality product on time and at a fair price. Potential foreign clients will want a list of the people who distribute and purchase your products in the United States so they can check out your reputation. To be in a position to do this takes time and work, so be patient: the international marketplace is willing to reward those who have paid their dues.

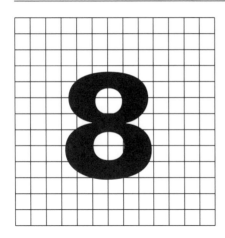

MEETING THE CHALLENGES OF THE FUTURE

CHAPTER OBJECTIVES
Upon completion of this chapter, you should be able to:
1. Chart the future in your chosen area of endeavor
2. Create a plan of action to prepare for the future

THE EVOLUTION OF THE GLOBAL MARKETPLACE

NAFTA, GATT, and the like are all designed to bring us closer to a truly free and open global marketplace. This evolution has been slow and rather painful at times, but it is inexorable, free trade is coming, simply because it has to: it is just good business.

Thus, whatever you are doing, it is likely that the market will expand throughout the course of your career. It is imperative that you prepare for the inevitable changes so that you will not be left behind.

An honest assessment of your current skills and the demands of the future is very much in order. If you are going to be rendered obsolete in the near future, make the requisite changes. Go back to school, learn a new skill, affiliate with a forward-looking organization. In short, do whatever it takes.

Futurists make projections concerning conditions that will exist down the road. There have been some remarkably prescient people down through the years (Jules Verne's stories come to mind), in and out of business.

NAFTA's original backers qualify as accurate futurists. Despite being denigrated by a wide variety of people, they persevered, and the agreement won out. Toward the end of NAFTA's first year, the nations represented at the hemispheric economic summit unanimously agreed to free trade throughout the Americas by 2005.

President Clinton, in an address to the gathering, spoke about a free trade zone stretching "from Alaska to Argentina."

NAFTA's future augurs well for you. Free trade throughout the Americas means that there will be a need for more internationally inclined workers, managers, consultants, and entrepreneurs. These will be people who have prepared themselves by learning Spanish (including business Spanish) and/or Portuguese and by studying the histories and cultures of the countries with which they want to do business.

PREPARING FOR NEW OPPORTUNITIES

Again, the bulk of the international careers will be here in the United States, but worldwide travel opportunities will abound.

> Management consulting is growing by 20 percent annually in the United States and even faster overseas. With the tremendous surge of business activity in Europe, accompanied by increased global competition and uncertainty, management consulting will be in even bigger demand. MBAs from top American or European business schools are the most likely to get into an international management consulting firm. Language and experience abroad will be expected.[1]

Dr. Bob Sanborn—quoted above—writes a regular feature, "The International Career Adviser," in *Transitions Abroad*. This publication is a highly useful tool for Americans who aspire to work overseas. Here are some of Dr. Sanborn's recent features that may be of interest to you: "International Career Trends" (September/October 1993); "Where the Jobs Are" (January/February 1994); "NAFTA and International Jobs" (May/June 1994).

In his article on NAFTA, Sanborn makes a critical point:

> Fluency in Spanish will not guarantee you a job. The key to success is to demonstrate that in addition to speaking Spanish you have other skills that will prove valuable to your prospective employer: knowledge and experience with the culture picked up through a summer job or study abroad, hard business skills not easily found in Mexico, or contacts developed through experiences abroad.[2]

Dr. Sanborn's words echo what we have heard elsewhere. Thorough preparation—and language training is only a part of it—is required before you can seriously contend for positions in the international sector. Experience, contacts, expertise, and cultural awareness are also important elements. One way to gain experience is through volunteering, which is something we looked at earlier. For more suggestions, I suggest reading Will Cantrell and Francine Modderno's article, "Volunteering Abroad" (*Transitions Abroad*, September/October 1993). Another informative article is "Work Abroad: The Key Resources" (*Transitions Abroad*, July/August 1994).

For further information on this publication, write to:

> *Transitions Abroad*
> 18 Hulst Road
> P.O. Box 1300
> Amherst, MA 01004–1300

---

[1] Bob Sanborn, "Working in Europe," *Transitions Abroad*, November/December 1994, 65.

[2] Bob Sanborn, "NAFTA and International Jobs," *Transitions Abroad*, May/June 1994, 61.

NAFTA opens up a great many opportunities for positions in this hemisphere. These jobs will go to individuals who are experienced experts, so it is essential that you refrain from looking for a quick entry and instead prepare yourself for the long haul.

One way of assessing your readiness for international employment is to take the test in the appendix to this book. It will give you a good idea of your geographical, cultural, and historical awareness.

Your linguistic skills also need to be appraised realistically. To what extent can you really function in another language? Can you, solely using that language,

- Order a meal?
- Book transportation and lodging?
- Discuss a medical problem?
- Interface with local managers and personnel at a job site?
- Discuss your firm's products and services?
- Negotiate a contract (with the exception of the work that can only be performed by an attorney)?
- Write a detailed instructional memo?
- Write typical business letters?
- Discuss history, world affairs, and the global economy in detail?

The more times you were able to answer "yes" to the above, the better your prospects are for a career in international business.

THE EFFECTS OF FREER TRADE AND NEW TECHNOLOGY

People all over the world are excited by the prospects of freer trade. This is what one international manager had to say when asked whether NAFTA and GATT are harbingers of truly free trade on a global basis:

> GATT is an agreement among 117[3] countries that governs the conduct of international trade through a continuing process of trade liberalization: NAFTA and AFTA (ASEAN Free Trade Area) are regional free trade groupings that operate under the GATT umbrella. The Eighth Uruguay Round has certainly made advances in the direction of freer trade: lower tariffs in both developed and developing countries; conversion of non-tariff barriers to tariff equivalents; reduction of farm and export subsidies; and phase out of import quotas. As the successful conclusion of the Uruguay Round may reduce the preferential tariff advantages of AFTA members, the ASEAN economic ministers have agreed to speed up full implementation of the Common Effective Preferential Tariff (CEPT) scheme to January 1, 2003 (as against the original timetable of January 1, 2008). This will spur greater intra-ASEAN trade, lower costs of ASEAN-sourced raw material inputs, encourage joint ventures and cross-border investment tie-ups, and weaken country-specific advantages arising from tariff differentials.

---

[3] The number has since changed and is likely to continue to do so.

There will be losers as well as gainers. H. Ross Perot warns, for instance, that NAFTA pits American workers against Mexican workers, and GATT will pit American workers against those of China, India, and Pakistan, where labor is even cheaper than in Mexico. Concerns are also voiced in the Philippines, focusing on the lack of competitiveness in certain domestic industries like textiles and sugar production, and on the need for safety nets or even outright postponement of GATT ratification. The Philippine government also stands to lose revenues when tariffs fall. On the whole, however, the consensus in government and business circles is that GATT and AFTA will indeed bring about an increasingly liberalized trade environment, causing some economic dislocation but opening up new business opportunities, more efficient resource use and allocation, and a wider choice of products.[4]

Presidents, prime ministers, bankers, and corporate executives all over the world are optimistic about the future. There will be growing pains, though, and it is naive and counterproductive to pretend otherwise. We are hard pressed to find a business day when the papers do not tell of at least one major firm "downsizing." Many of the layoffs are due to changes in the international marketplace. Real people are suffering major upheaval in their lives because of these changes.

Technology is also taking its toll. While technical advances are a boon to manufacturers and consumers alike, they frequently mean the end of the (career) line for unskilled and semiskilled workers and the managers who supervise them.

Steel yourself for a lifetime of continuous training, in order to remain employable. Job skills and knowledge, in addition to the language and cultural training we have discussed and continuing to gain on-the-job experience are all challenges you will face throughout your career.

In many cases, you will be vying for positions in direct competition with not only your fellow Americans, but the best people available from all over the world. Truly free trade means that individuals and organizations will be "free" to fail as well as to succeed.

YOU AND THE FUTURE

Reality-based education is critically important if you are to prepare properly to compete in a global job market and, given the rapid and radical changes that are occurring, even hitherto "domestic" positions are going global. So, you need to face the fact that the world of work will not be as protective or lucrative as it was in the past.

In many cases, you will work harder for less money and job security. Contract work, even in management, is a highly likely possibility.

Having said that, I remain optimistic about the future, at least insofar as the prospects for people who are willing to learn and grow are concerned. In short, if you are not afraid of change, and you are willing to keep studying so that your skills continue to grow, your future will be a bright one.

---

[4] Jimmy Ong, personal correspondence.

You will work for and with people from all over the world. In the process, you will have an opportunity to test yourself not only in the commercial market, but also in the much more interesting marketplace of ideas.

You will discover differences between yourself and others that will teach you a great deal about why our world is the way that it is. In the process, you will share your own insights with others and contribute to their knowledge concerning our country.

These communications will greatly reduce the sweeping, ignorant generalizations of the past that have led to fear, hatred, and even war.

So, you will be not only a worker, manager, or entrepreneur, you will also be an ambassador! You will move freely from one culture to another, enjoying much more flexibility than all but a handful of people who have preceded you.

Travel, new experiences, new friendships, and greater understanding are all benefits that will accrue to you if you are willing to take the time and make the effort.

Start small. Begin at home. Progress logically. Make your career desires known through networking. Realize that you will never know everything, but delight in making the quest for an ever-increasing body of personal and professional knowledge!

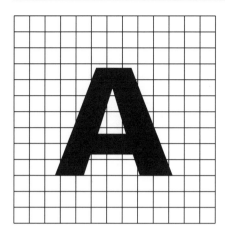

APPENDIX A
OUR "FOREIGN SERVICE EXAM"

Introduction: The premise of this book is that the vast majority of people in the United States are ill-prepared for working in the international sector. Language skills are of course important, but it is also useful to look at how much you know about the world in general. You should know the answers to the questions on this exam. Take the test honestly, and see how you do. The answer key is at the end of the exam. Please note that the information being tested may be readily located in newspapers, magazines, and history and business books (including some I have quoted and/or recommended in this book). CNN, NPR, and PBS stations are also superb sources of international news.

In an era of international trade agreements, changes will inevitably take place. This includes expansion of trading partnerships among countries through mergers and new member countries. However, although a given organization may change its name, it is still useful to know what it was originally called.

1. Name the Benelux nations:

2. What is the capital of Nicaragua?

3. Taiwan used to be known as _____.

4. Who was Simon Bolivar, and where was he born?

5. The Versailles Treaty officially ended which war?

6. Who was the "Sun King"?
   What famous structure did he build?

7. Suriname is located between what two countries?

8. The Falklands War was fought between what countries?

9. What countries border Panama?

10. Where was Maximilian of Mexico born?

11. Which country backed Maximilian by providing him with troops and money?

12. Who was president of the United States when Maximilian became emperor?

13. In _____, those in authority cannot admit lack
        (name of country)
    of knowledge or mistakes for fear of losing _____.

14. What is the "gray" market?

15. When did the Russian Revolution begin?

16. Who ruled Spain as a dictator prior to the restoration of the present monarchy?

17. Define hard currency:

18. Jose Rizal is a major national hero in what country?

19. What is the primary language in Brazil?

20. Where is the United Nations located?

21. What is the title of the individual who heads the United Nations?

22. Mecca is located in which country?

23. The Gulf War began when _____
                                       (name of country)
    invaded and occupied _____.
                                  (name of country)

24. _____ was the President of the United States.
    (name of person)
    when the Camp David summit between Israel and Egypt was held.
    President _____ headed the Egyptian delegation,
                    (name)
    while the Israelis were led by _____.
                                          (name)

25. In 1997, which British colony will become part of China?

26. Liege is located in _____.
                          (name of country)

27. The capital of Paraguay is _____.
                                    (name)

28. What is an "ECU"?

29. The capital of Haiti is _____.
                              (name of city)

30. The *cruzeiro* is the monetary unit of _____.
                                              (name of country)

31. The capital of Thailand is _____.
                                  (name of city)

32. The capital of Poland is _____.
                                (name of city)

33. The Tierra del Fuego is located at the tip of _____.
                                                    (name of continent)

34. Marakesh is located in _____.
                              (name of country)

35. Maracaibo is located in _____.
                              (name of country)

36. The "Tonkin Gulf Incident" is associated with the
    _____ War.
          (name)

37. _____ is the capital of Canada.
          (name of city)

38. Montreal is located in the province of _____.
                                              (name)

39. The battleship *Bismarck* was sunk during _____.

40. The Uffizi Museum is located in _____.
     (names of city and country)

41. Heinrich _____ of Germany and Jean Paul
     (last name)
     _____ both won the Nobel Prize for
     (last name)
     _____.
     (category)

42. The primary residence for the ruling monarch of the United
     Kingdom is _____.
     (name of structure)

43. The capital of Peru is _____.
     (name of city)

44. The city of Ismailia is a city in _____.
     (name of country)
     You'll find it near the _____ Canal.
     (name)

45. The Prado is an _____ museum. It is located in
     _____.
     (names of city and country)

46. The term OPEC is associated with _____.
     (commodity)

47. Margaret _____ was the _____
     (last name)   (title)
     of _____ during the Falklands War.
     (name of country)

48. _____ composed the opera *The Magic Flute*.
     (last name)

49. Kabuki is a type of theater in _____.
     (name of country)

50. Kabul is the capital of _____.
     (name of country)

51. Toronto is located in the Canadian province of _____.
     (name)

52. The largest city in Manitoba is _____.
（name)

53. Lufthansa is the national airline of _____.
(name of country)

54. The initials that Royal Dutch Airlines is known by are:

55. Benito _____ ruled Italy before
(last name)
(and during most of) World War II. His followers were called

_____.
(term)

56. _____, wrote two major political books:
(first and last name)
1984 and *Animal* _____.
(name)

57. Montreal is on the _____.
(name of river)

58. Medellin is located in _____.
(name of country)

59. Two capital cities, _____, Argentina and
(name)
_____, Uruguay are very close to each other.
(name)
Their nation's borders are divided by the _____.
(name of river)

60. Ho Chi Minh City used to be known as _____.
(name)

61. Hudson Bay is located in _____.
(name of country)

62. Sicily is an island in the _____ Sea.
(name)

63. Edmonton is the capital of the province of _____.
(name)

64. Monaco is bordered by _____.
(names of countries)

65. The capital of Romania is _____.
(name)

66. Nassau is the capital of _____.
(name)

67. Santo _____ is the capital of
(name)
_____. This nation shares the same island
(name)
with another country, _____.
(name)

68. The most famous river in Egypt is the _____.
(name)

69. Bogota is the capital of _____.
(name)

70. The _____ Strait separates which U.S. state
from the former Soviet Union? _____

71. Camaguey is a province in _____.
(name of country)

72. Jalisco is a state in the country of _____.
(name)

73. Amman is the capital of _____.
(name)

74. Bangalore is located in _____.
(name of country)

75. _____ is the primary language spoken in
(name)
Istanbul.

76. The *baht* is _____'s monetary unit.
(name of country)

77. Chad is located in _____.
(continent)

78. Kaiser _____ ruled Germany until he abdicated
(name)
during _____.
(name of war)

79. Kurt _____ headed the United Nations, and was
       (name)
    subsequently president of _____.
                                    (country)

80. Which 20th century dictator was an athletic star and a practicing
    attorney? (Hint: He is famous for saying, "History will absolve
    me.")

81. Identify the Maquis.

82. The capital of Sweden is _____.
                                     (name)

83. *La aduana* is the _____ term for
                            (name of language)
    _____.

84. Budapest is the capital of _____.

85. Bergen and Stavenger are located on the coast of
    _____.

86. Miguel Aleman served as president of _____.

87. Making the _____ at least once is vitally
                      (term)
    important to devout _____.
                              (religion)

88. Scottish kings were crowned at _____.
                                          (location)

89. Algiers is on the _____.
                          (body of water)

90. Reykjavik is the capital of _____.

91. The United States boycotted the _____
                                            (city)
    Olympics during the administration of President _____.
                                                          (name)

92. Tegucigalpa is the capital of _____.

93. The former capital of Brazil is _____.
                                          (name)

94. The capital of Finland is _____.
                                              (name)

95. Copenhagen is located in _____.

96. *Wagon-lits* is the _____ term for
                                        (language)

     _____.

97. Sao Paulo is a major city in _____.
                                                      (country)

98. Their defeat at Dien Bien Phu ended the reign of the
     _____ in _____.
                  (name)   (country)

99. Cork is a major port city in _____.
                                                      (country)

100. _____ is the capital of Puerto Rico.

Answers

1. Belgium, The Netherlands, Luxembourg.
2. Managua.
3. Formosa.
4. A revolutionary leader who helped to liberate South America from Spain. Caracas, Venezuela.
5. World War I.
6. Louis XIV of France. The Palace of Versailles.
7. Guyana and French Guyana.
8. Argentina and the United Kingdom.
9. Costa Rica, Colombia.
10. Austria.
11. France.
12. Abraham Lincoln.
13. China. Face.
14. Parallel importation.
15. 1917.
16. Francisco Franco.
17. Readily convertible money.
18. The Philippines.

19. Portuguese.
20. New York City.
21. Secretary General.
22. Saudi Arabia.
23. Iraq. Kuwait.
24. Jimmy Carter. Sadat. (Prime Minister) Menachem Begin.
25. Hong Kong.
26. Belgium.
27. Asuncion.
28. A European Currency Unit.
29. Port Au Prince.
30. Brazil.
31. Bangkok.
32. Warsaw.
33. South America.
34. Morocco.
35. Venezuela.
36. Vietnam.
37. Ottawa.
38. Quebec.
39. World War II.
40. Florence, Italy.
41. Böll. Sartre. Literature.
42. Buckingham Palace.
43. Lima.
44. Egypt. Suez.
45. Art. Madrid, Spain.
46. Oil.
47. Thatcher. Prime Minister. Great Britain.
48. Mozart.
49. Japan.
50. Afghanistan.
51. Ontario.
52. Winnepeg.
53. Germany.
54. KLM.
55. Mussolini. Facists.
56. George Orwell. *Farm*.
57. St. Lawrence.

58. Colombia.
59. Buenos Aires. Montevideo. Rio de la Plata.
60. Saigon.
61. Canada.
62. Mediterranean.
63. Alberta.
64. Italy and France.
65. Bucharest.
66. The Bahamas.
67. Domingo. The Dominican Republic. Haiti.
68. Nile.
69. Colombia.
70. Bering. Alaska.
71. Cuba.
72. Mexico.
73. Jordan.
74. India.
75. Turkish.
76. Thailand.
77. Africa.
78. Wilhelm. World War I.
79. Waldheim. Austria.
80. Fidel Castro.
81. The French Underground during World War II.
82. Stockholm.
83. Spanish. Customs (prior to entering a country).
84. Hungary.
85. Norway.
86. Mexico.
87. Hajj (also haj). Muslims.
88. Scone.
89. Mediterranean.
90. Iceland.
91. Moscow. Carter.
92. Honduras.
93. Rio de Janiero.
94. Helsinki.
95. Denmark.
96. French. Sleeping cars.

97. Brazil.

98. French. Vietnam.

99. Ireland.

100. San Juan.

Scoring: Allow one point for each complete correct answer. You must answer all parts of the multifaceted questions in order to receive the point.

90–100:   Excellent. Now, what do you really know about all of these people, places and things?

80–89:   Good, but more study is needed.

79 or less: You have a shaky grasp of the world around you. You need more study before you seriously consider seeking work in the international sector.

If you are unhappy with your score, do not waste time railing against past teachers who failed you even while they were "passing" you. Instead, vow to learn the answers to these (and many other) questions on your own.

If you did well, congratulations! You have shown that you have a good foundation to build on.

Either way, the world is large and very diverse, and a lifetime is not long enough to learn everything there is to know about it. Happily, languages, cultures, currencies, alliances, the arts, politics, and history are all fascinating areas of study so, although a lot of work is required, it will be enjoyable.

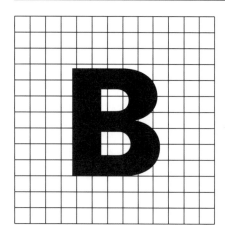

APPENDIX B
ON COMMUNITY COLLEGES

Author's note: Although I teach at a four-year college, I had the privilege of attending and graduating from a community college. I learned at that time what enormous contributions two-year colleges can and do make. I am not alone in feeling this way, as the following remarks delivered by United States Secretary of Labor Robert B. Reich attest.*

I've said it before—and I'll say it again this morning—community colleges are American heroes. But they fall into that special category. They're *unsung* heroes. And I've been wondering why.

Over the last several months, I think I've begun to figure it out. Community colleges are pioneers. And here's what can happen with pioneers: we sometimes don't notice them because *we* remain fixed in one spot while *they* chart new territories. Community colleges are blazing new trails, while everyone else is still deciding what to do next.

And, as in most endeavors, California is taking the lead. Your colleges together comprise one of the largest education systems in the entire world. Nearly six percent of your citizens over the age of 18 are enrolled in community colleges, the second highest portion in the nation. The future often reaches California first. But Californians are also frequently the first to respond in innovative ways that the rest of the country can admire and emulate. California's community colleges are no exception.

For the past twenty months, President Clinton and his Administration have engaged in a mission very similar to your own. We've been trying to clear the obstacles that prevent too many Americans from leading full, productive lives.

* Transcript of Robert B. Reich's address to the California Community College Systems, Sacramento, California, September 29, 1994. Reprinted with permission.

That's no easy task. Clearing *these* obstacles takes more than brawn. It also takes brains. Indeed, we have to change the very way we *think* about the world. Until recently, Americans lived in an economy built on standardized mass production. Competitive advantage came from making more and more of the same thing at a cheaper and cheaper price. But now we live in a radically different economy—where competitive advantage grows from different roots.

America's best companies are realizing that most elements of their business can be replicated by competitors—machines, processes, raw materials, access to cheap labor around the world. The only thing that cannot be easily duplicated is workers—their skills, their creativity, their capacity to work together. A skilled, flexible workforce can create value in ways that matter in the marketplace. A skilled, flexible workforce can be a strategic trump card. A skilled, flexible workforce is the *only enduring competitive advantage*.

And that means we've got to use a different approach to prepare all Americans for work. Conventional thinking has had it that education, training, and retraining are distinct enterprises separated somehow by walls. Education is for kids. Education is books and blackboards and schoolrooms. Higher education is also education, but it's for the top slice of our population, those who are supposedly the highest among us. Training is a separate category altogether, something we provide to people we haven't deemed higher. We train these young men and women, and then send them on their way. But retraining is something different again. Retraining is reserved for the unlucky few who have lost jobs and now must get new ones.

The system that has emerged is less a system than it is a collection of loosely adjoined kingdoms whose walls are so high each one barely knows the other exists. And this set of walled territories confronts us at precisely the time the world economy's central feature is its capacity to *obliterate* walls of every kind. With the flick of a computer key, for example, information and capital can race through cyberspace, across national borders, unimpeded by walls of any sort. The wall between goods and services is falling in our new economy as more and more of the value of a product is embedded in related services delivered before it is manufactured and after it is sold. Walls can't even stop this speech, which is bouncing off a satellite somewhere in outer space—and then bouncing into your hotel ballroom 3000 miles from where I sit.

In this new boundary-less economy, what you earn depends on what you learn. And just as many of our best companies have responded to dynamism and change, so must our learning institutions. We can no longer think of education as something that happens to someone once, something that someone is subjected to once. Learning is not an event; it's a process. It doesn't occur; it continues. It doesn't start and stop; it goes and goes.

A system where schooling, higher education, and training are segmented no longer meets the needs of the American economy or the American workforce.... Community colleges offer long-term skill development that goes beyond the hit-or-miss, one-shot efforts that characterize many traditional training programs. In addition, community colleges often team with local businesses to provide the type of learning that will be most useful on the job. Students who attend community colleges understandably want some assurance that the time and money they devote will actually lead to a job, and community colleges' links to local employers deliver on that promise.

Community colleges also serve the women and men our current system frequently neglects: the older, so-called non-traditional, student. In fact, 37 percent of students in community colleges are 25 years or older, proving once again the commitment these institutions have to continuous learning. Nearly half of community colleges' part-time students are 25 years or older, demonstrating that a partial infrastructure is in place for a genuine system of lifelong learning that can upgrade a worker's skills throughout his or her career. And in the truest test of their value, community colleges are producing results. The median income of men with community college degrees is 26 percent higher than for those with only a high school diploma. Women who have graduated from community colleges have median incomes 33 percent higher than women with high school degrees alone.

I've seen this success with my own eyes. I've met countless people who are thriving largely because of the dedication and innovation of a community college. For example, I've met one young woman who went from unemployment to a good-paying position as an installation technician—and another, a single mother, who went from welfare to a job as a nurse.

Perhaps my favorite is the story of John Hahn. John had worked for Bell Aerospace for 28 years when defense downsizing eliminated his job. Since he hadn't looked for work in nearly three decades, and since the defense industry was shrinking, he decided he needed a new set of skills. Through the GATEWAY project, he enrolled in a telecommunications program at Niagara County Community College in New York. JTPA covered his tuition and books, and provided a travel allowance. Today, he is employed as a biomedical technician at a local hospital.

Many of you have seen similar stories unfold at your own colleges. And you've seen them unfold for an increasingly diverse population—for whom community colleges operate as an important point of entry into the workforce. Chabot Community College in Hayward, for example, has established the Puente Project, which is designed to help Latino young people enter the world of work, and which has spread to 30 other community colleges in California.

A constant theme of American history has been the challenge of forging unity out of diversity. Over and over, we have had to affirm our identity as one nation, even in the face of profound differences. We are at such a point once again. This time, though, the deepest divisions aren't based on race or on national origin or on geography. They're based on the ability of individuals to make their way in an increasingly turbulent economy.

Community colleges are helping millions make their way with confidence. That's why the President and I—and this entire Administration—are committed to assisting you with your mission. Thank you for your leadership. Let's continue to work together.

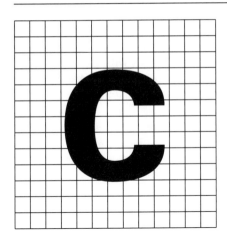

APPENDIX C
ON WORKING OVERSEAS—
THE VIEW FROM THE TOP

Jimmy Ong is a senior executive of a manufacturing and marketing company that is based in the Philippines and is expanding throughout Southeast Asia. I had the pleasure of interviewing him, and he had a great deal of valuable information to impart.

Q. Do you feel more comfortable having your company represented by local nationals around the world? If so, why?

A. Yes. As the company expands its international operations (we're now in Hong Kong, China, Indonesia, Vietnam, Guam, and Taiwan) it will experience a need for qualified technical and managerial talent that cannot be supplied by the parent firm in the Philippines. For now, Filipinos serve in many—but not all—key positions in these overseas operations, but this is simply because we have just acquired or started managing these ventures and need to understand them better, or because we need to install the requisite systems and technology.

But we realize that local nationals understand the local culture, language, markets, and business customs. The learning must happen on both sides: people in the parent company have to learn more about its host countries and markets and competition. The local nationals have to learn about the parent company's norms, standards, processes, and systems. At the end…the key positions in every operation should be occupied by the best qualified men or women, regardless of nationality. In a conference we held in the summer of 1994, the officer corps identified management development as a critical task and stated explicitly that management development covers all employees, regardless of nationality.

Q. What's the best way for Americans to prepare for working in the international sector?

A. Preparation will come to naught unless one begins with three attributes: 1) A refusal to assume that whatever worked in one's previous company or country will work just as well in the next; 2) a willingness to listen and learn; and 3) a sense of humor.

This observation applies not just to Americans, but to anyone working in a new environment. Some of our horror stories have to do with managers joining us after impressive careers in American companies, and assuming that, given their credentials, they could make brilliant unilateral decisions which would leave the natives gasping in awe.

On the matter of social preparation, one would do well to 1) learn about the host country; and 2) learn about the company. The employee's spouse should take part in this preparatory activity, as she/he is bound to experience a greater feeling of loneliness and vulnerability than the employee, whose work environment creates a natural network and source of social support. It goes without saying that a crash course of 15 lessons of spoken Mandarin is hopelessly inadequate as preparation for an assignment in Shanghai; the ideal preparation would entail staying in the country and learning about the customs, history, business laws, and so forth before being given a full-time job in it.

A number of educational institutions try to provide something of this nature as part of their MBA programs. The Wharton Institute offers month-long study tours of China and Japan, and a chance to work in teams studying actual problems in individual companies. The Haas School of Business at UC Berkeley offers summer consulting projects in Indonesia and Malaysia. The Australian National University offers courses in eight Asian languages, and after three semesters of study on campus, a 12-week period of supervised work outside a participant's country of origin.

Q. You've seen Americans abroad. What do they need to work on to make themselves better representatives of their country?

A. I don't think that Americans working abroad should begin with the objective of making themselves better representatives of their country, unless they are in the foreign service and therefore explicitly mandated to represent the United States' official position. The challenge is for Americans to make themselves more effective performers in that foreign milieu. Effectiveness may require downplaying the official American line. The following may help:

1. Develop a healthy curiosity about the host country: its culture, its customs, its religion, and its history. Bone up a bit before going, and ask questions upon getting there. Your hosts will generally be pleased to talk about themselves, their festivals, and their legends.

But remember that where a country's history has intersected with that of the United States, there may be a residue of misunderstanding or resentment.

2. Make friends among the locals. There will be a temptation, where a small American community exists, to become a part of that enclave. But—even if it takes a bit longer—one should also cultivate friends among the locals. This advice also applies to the spouse and children.

3. Build for the long term. Look beyond the immediate transaction or business equation. There is a great deal that an Asian will never tell you at the first meeting, or second, or third. Respect that reticence, and display no impatience.

A complete list of titles in our extensive *Opportunities* series

VGM Career Horizons
a division of *NTC Publishing Group*
4255 West Touhy Avenue
Lincolnwood, Illinois 60646–1975